Praise for
Brilliant Babies, Powerful Adults

"These techniques and strategies can dramatically increase our children's intellect and also help us to create powerful and loving relationships."
— John Gray, PhD
National Bestselling Author, *Men Are from Mars, Women Are from Venus*

"I wish we had this book when we were raising our five children. Your child has unlimited potential. Read this book and become an inspired parent with a fulfilled child."
— Bernie S. Siegal, M.D.
National Bestselling Author of *Love, Medicine & Miracles*

"Dr. Mike reminds us that when we believe in the power of love and that the mind has no limits, that nothing is impossible."
— Gerald G. Jampolsky, MD
Author, *Love Is Letting Go of Fear*

"Dr. Mike's research, his extraordinary experience, and his love for the truth are beautifully woven together in this book...His method of fetal intellectual stimulation during pregnancy will revolutionize the educational process. You will learn how to treat the primary cause of human conflict. Dr. Mike's book is very timely. I'm going to see that all my friends receive a copy; I suggest you do the same."
— Bob Proctor
Author, *You Were Born Rich;*
Chairman, LifeSuccess Institute

"Dr. John Mike's book will help parents to develop an extremely positive bond with their children. This bond by itself can eliminate many of the problems that face parents and children, and improve the quality of family life.
— Richard D. Allen, PhD
Director, Counseling and Psychological Services
University of California, Santa Cruz

"I hope this books finds its way into the hands of many parents. The information it contains is sound and helpful."
— Richard D. Carson
Author, *Taming Your Gremlin*

"*Brilliant Babies, Powerful Adults* is a must-read for expecting parents. A powerful book that will help many."
— Margot Robinson
Author, *The Peaceful Soul Within:*
Reflective Steps Towards Awareness

"A simple yet dynamic way to change your life. If everyone practiced these principles, the world would be a much happier place."
— Paul Peevy
Motivational Speaker, Storyteller to Children,
Standup Comic

"I know for a fact that John Mike, MD is committed 100% to being and teaching the transformative message that his book brings to our times. Take action and dare to evoke that loving power in your children, yourself, and everyone you come in touch with. I am delighted to be his colleague."
— Ron Lopez, MD
Diplomate American Academy of Child Psychiatry

"'Brilliant' is not only the title of the book, it is exactly what the book is. It is basic common sense for a simple way of life to Brilliance. If you care anything at all about the baby you are about to have, then this book is a must."
— Kathy Buckley
Hearing-impaired Comedienne, and
Advocate for Children's Education

"As a parent/stepparent of ten children, I strongly advise anyone thinking of having children to read this inspirational, practical book as a first step in the process. Or if you want to make changes in your own life, use the tools to reprogram your subconscious now, and have the happiness you want."
— Ivan G. Burnell
Author, *The Power of Positive Doing*

"Dr. Mike reaches into the psyche to pull out what it takes to better our own lives and, more importantly, the lives of our children. For anyone dealing with personal issues, searching to find answers to human development, or aspiring to nurture children with love, *Brilliant Babies, Powerful Adults* is a must-read."

— Dave Pelzer
Author, *A Child Called It*

In this time of the dysfunstional family unit, Dr. Mike empowers us to intellectually, physically, spiritually, and emotionally nourish our children. He helps us believe that we can and will create brilliant, loved babies. This book is a must for health professionals caring for women and children.

— Kimberly Krepp, M.D.
Clinical Faculty in Family Practice
Memorial Hospital, Chattanooga, Tennessee

Dedication

To my father Joseph Ablen Mike, Sr.
You taught me that I could achieve anything
when I focus my mind. You began teaching
me this as a child when you lifted me off the
ground while I was holding onto your hair.
You said pain is all in our mind.
I no longer believe your words are true—I
know they are and thank you.

To my mother for her continued love and support.
Through your example, I learned the true meaning of
love.

To my wife who taught me many great insights into
myself. Your endless energy, unlimited support, and love
have carried me through this project. You have been my
greatest teacher and fan.

I love you all, John Maron Mike, M.D.

Many blessings
to you & your family as
you grow in love & light
of understanding.
Love, Susan Mohn *mo*

BRILLIANT BABIES
POWERFUL ADULTS
Awaken the Genius Within

To The
Lizano Family,
You are incredible lights
To the faith, keep on shining.
Love, John Mike *ms*

Satori Press International
1831 North Belcher Road, Suite F4
Clearwater, FL 34625
phone (813) 669-3911; fax (813) 669-3813

To purchase additional copies, please visit your favorite local bookstore. To inquire about bulk discounts for multiple orders, contact the publisher at (813) 669-3911.

Bookstores and wholesalers, please contact Access Publishers Network, 6893 Sullivan Road, Grawn, MI 49637; phone (800) 345-0096; fax (800) 950-9793

Front Cover Photography ©
Baby-Weeks/The Stock Broker LLC
Adult-G. Bartholomew/Westlight.

Printed in the United States of America.

Library of Congress Catalog Card Number: 96-69103

Brilliant Babies, Powerful Adults: Awaken the Genius Within. By John Mike, MD.

ISBN 0-9644294-2-x
First Edition

10 9 8 7 6 5 4 3 2 1

Contents

Foreword

Wow! Read this great book and meet the most important person in the world—You! *Brilliant Babies, Powerful Adults* teaches you how to effectively use your own mind power.

I loved this book and I think you will too. Why? Because each of us has a mind, and each of us has a purpose about which to get passionate. Dr. John Mike teaches you the "who," so the "how" becomes effortless effort. He makes it an easy, fast, insightful, and delightful read.

Master your mind and your emotions, and you've got your life and your future mastered. Dr. Mike simply shares proven ways to bring out our imprisoned genius abilities, become illumined, and astonish ourselves at our vast potential.

As you read, come to understand, ponder, and use the dynamic principles in this book, you will become ever more brilliant, powerful, influential, and beneficial to yourself and others. Enjoy reading!

— Mark Victor Hansen
co-author of the #1 *New York Times* best-selling series, *Chicken Soup for the Soul*

Acknowledgments

If time allowed me, I could write an entire book on all of the friends, colleagues, and professors who have influenced my education and my life. I wish to devote this time to all of these individuals, at Youngstown State University, The University of Toledo, The Medical College of Ohio, and The University of South Florida Medical Center, who contributed their great effort and spirit through their gifts of knowledge.

Rick and Carolynn Crandall of Select Press have provided incredible professionalism, support, and phenomenal commitment in their communication with me during the process of editing this book. Their staff and team of editors have performed a remarkable job throughout this entire procedure.

I wish to thank Bruce Edson, MD, and Michael Poff, LCSW, for their contributions in editing and critiquing the material in this book.

I also thank the patients who, though their names have been changed for the sake of confidentiality, have given permission to share their stories. We have all learned from your experiences.

Finally, I would like to thank my wife Susan for her insights, energy, contributions, editing, and unlimited support throughout this entire process.

Preface

My Quest

This book is the culmination of decades of study and self-reflection. I am a child, adolescent, and adult psychiatrist currently working as the Medical Director of a residential treatment center for adolescent females. I work in both acute psychiatric care and residential settings, and have a private outpatient practice. The road that I traveled to arrive here has been fascinating and is what this book is about.

The Early Years and Education

I am the third child of four, of parents who were first generation immigrants. Hard working, moral, ethical, and religious, they instilled these values into their children. I spent the summers since the age of seven working in my father and uncle's business, ACME Steak Co. Inc. in Youngstown, Ohio.

I completed my Bachelors degree in economics with a philosophy and criminal justice minor. I then studied for a Masters degree at Johns Hopkins University School of Advanced International Studies (SAIS). After completing my first semester my father asked me to return to the business.

Loss Leads To A Shift In Career

I was a devoted son, and felt guilty when I was not helping out in the business. So, motivated by guilt, I returned. Nine months later my father died suddenly, two days before Christmas, 1983. He was 58 years old and died from what I now believe was a pulmonary embolism which led to a massive heart attack.

There was a difficult transition period for everyone but through this challenge, I decided to leave the business and enter another profession. Many relatives still worked in the business so my leaving would not adversely affect the company.

I looked at my life and decided that of all the things I enjoyed, I loved to help people and I loved mathematics. I had worked with several lawyers after my father's death and ruled out this profession for myself. I was also dating a young lady who was one of four sisters: two had graduated from medical school and two were currently in medical school. At the age of 24, I decided to become a doctor.

Medical School

To apply to medical school, I needed two years of pre-med classes. This was two years of chemistry, one year each of biology and physics, and all the labs. My guidance counselor suggested that it would take two years to complete these studies. Since I was already 24 years old—older than the typical pre-med student—I desired to complete the courses in one year, summer to summer. The guidance counselor stated that it was a serious mistake to try to complete this course of work in one year because, if my grades were not excellent, I would not get into medical school.

I finished the pre-med courses in one year with a GPA of 4.0, took the entrance exam, and was accepted into all the medical schools to which I applied. Four years later, I graduated from medical school and five years later I finished my residency and Child and Adolescent fellowship in Psychiatry.

In medical school I loved learning everything having to do with the brain. I decided to enter the field of medicine that focuses on the brain and the entire belief and behavior system of a person.

A Burning Desire

I had one burning desire: to understand why I was the only one of four children to have academically excelled. My immediate family and other relatives asked the same question of me. I had no idea. My siblings had all entered college, but I was the only one to graduate (and graduated summa cum laude). Then I went on to postgraduate studies and medical school. It did not seem like genetics alone could explain the intellectual differences since we all had the same parents and similar genetic material.

When I thought about our upbringing, one difference did surface, although at the time I did not know what it meant.

I had an uncle named "Woody" (Wadih Mike) who had entered this country just after I was born. He "adopted" me as his favorite child since I was the baby in the family at the time. I had been told by him and others how he would visit me every day, carry me around, sing, and talk to me constantly—and how I used to wet on his shirt. I guess I felt comfortable!

A New Set Of Questions

I began to wonder if—because of this early stimulation—my brain developed differently, to give me the intellectual capacity to achieve what I have academically.

As I pondered this hypothesis, it raised a series of questions about early stimulation, the answers to which we were not taught during my medical and psychiatric training. I began to question the parents of children with IQs in the superior or very superior range. As the evidence accumulated, I now have no doubt that early stimulation dramatically improves intellectual functioning way beyond anything we can imagine at this point.

* * * * *

This is only the beginning of the potential of this book. We can raise our children to be brilliant, and create in them a powerful and positive self-image and subconscious mind. In doing this, we can also gain an understanding of ourselves and our issues.

I discuss emotions and how to take control of our lives by creating the emotions we desire. We can tap into our unlimited potential and live in a state of happiness and abundance instead of fear and lack.

I loved writing this book. The thought of people gaining awareness and insight into themselves from reading this book is incredible. If the information in this book is applied, there will be a dramatic shift in our world that has never been known. We will create Brilliant Babies and Powerful Adults.

The Beginning...

I enter the waiting room looking forward to seeing my next patient. As I approach the family, a young boy confidently stands up. He is dressed well, with his shirt buttoned up, dress jeans, and hair parted on the side. He speaks first which surprises me, "You must be Doctor Mike."

"Yes, I am—and you must be Jason." An unusual beginning of a psychiatric evaluation for an eight-year-old boy.

As the process unfolded, it was clear that Jason was a very intelligent young boy. Prior neuropsychological testing provided by the parents confirmed this. Jason possessed an IQ above 140 (the average range is 90 to 110).

Asking A Different Question

As I gathered the usual background information from the parents, I asked several questions about the boy's early intellectual stimulation. These questions were born out of my desire to understand intelligence and how we can influence it, rather than accept the idea that it is determined mostly by genetics.

Early Stimulation

The mother replied, "I read to him daily when I was pregnant and after he was born. I thought it would make him smarter, and I think it did."

Many parents are not sure why they do it, but they are inspired to develop the relationship—the bond between themselves and the fetus. They also believe that their child can hear them and may begin to learn.

Another mother, whose daughter Jessica possessed an IQ in the very superior range (above 130), reported that she read to her two-year-old son while she was pregnant with Jessica. After her daughter's birth, she placed Jessica alongside her son and read to them both on a daily basis.

> *"Recent research into the early childhood experiences of unusually talented adults has revealed that their early childhood environments were exceptionally supportive and enriched...[Research findings] strongly suggest that parental support plays a critical role in a child's eventually achieving his or her full intellectual, artistic, or athletic potential."*
>
> —Tom and Nancy Biracree,
> *The Parents' Book of Facts: Child Development from Birth to Age Five*

Change The World...
One Child At A Time

These parents have found a key to their children's development. Such early stimulation can dramatically improve intellectual development and maximize the incredible potential of the human brain.

Brain Development

By the 16th day after conception, the brain has started forming. By the sixth month, all the brain cells are essentially in place. In this book, you will learn how you can start affecting intellectual growth during pregnancy. The possibility of increasing the IQ of our children through early stimulation is just a part of what this book will explain.

Our Children And Ourselves

I'm a child, adolescent, and adult psychiatrist. One of my roles is Medical Director of a treatment facility funded by the state of Florida for teenaged girls (ages 13 to 18). In this role, I see many teenagers who have not had a stimulating, nurturing, and supportive environment.

These girls are just one step away from prison. At the treatment facility, we help girls who have drug addictions; who have prostituted themselves; and who have committed assault and battery, grand theft, and numerous other crimes.

Most of these young women come from abusive or neglectful families. Some have only borderline intelligence, have been homeless, and are victims of sexual abuse and other traumatic and challenging events.

Positive Bonding Needed

A lack of early stimulation inhibited many of these girls from reaching their maximum intellectual potential. Their emotional bonding was also impaired, and positive role models were lacking in their lives. Emotional bonding with an adult, and having positive role models, are vital for healthy development.

In this book, you will learn how to create this powerful emotional bond and understand how it influences development. I will explain how to become a powerful and positive role model. I will also show how human development proceeds in stages, each stage building on the achievements of the prior stage.

Read On—Even If You Don't Have Children

You will also discover the power of the subconscious mind, how it forms, and how you can influence it. You can create a powerful and positive subconscious mind in yourself.

You can begin to direct your life and achieve your greatest desires, instead of just accepting what life brings. You can propel your life in

the direction of your dreams, instead of finding yourself powerless to escape your old habits and behaviors.

Learning The Basics

We can achieve extraordinary growth by learning some fundamental things about our lives. Too often, these are things we were never taught directly, but were supposed to "pick up" along the way. These skills can make us more successful in life and help us realize our true abundance. These include:

- how to have a positive attitude
- the power of goal setting
- how to become a leader
- how to attract the things you desire
- how to develop powerful and loving relationships

Growing Within

We can increase the passion and happiness of our lives through a greater understanding of our own conflicts. Our conflicts exist not just in our intimate relationships, but with every person in our lives, including our children.

> *"Everything that irritates us about others can lead us to an understanding of ourselves."*
> —Carl Jung

We all have room to grow. Unless we work through our problems, they will continue to interfere with our daily lives.

You will learn to understand how and why your

conflicts formed and how to recognize them. This book will show you how you can rise above these conflicts by stopping "preframed" old "scripts" from controlling your actions and reactions—and begin to live in the present.

How This Book Can Help You

The first goal of this book is to show you what's possible to help yourself. I will uncover many ways you can improve the lives of your children and yourself. I want to show you how much is possible—*inspire you*—and get you started on a path to self-understanding and mastery.

Your Children—The Future

In the first part of the book, I'll discuss the beginning for all of us—how to help your new baby develop his or her full potential.

Early stimulation for the brain is key to maximizing your baby's intellectual potential. You can add 20 to 40 points to your baby's IQ. You will also learn insightful parenting techniques that will help your children develop powerful and positive self-images and subconscious minds. I'll spend much of my time with you discussing these concepts and techniques.

By raising one generation to realize its full potential, we could change the world immediately. Think what a generation of emotionally healthy, extremely intelligent young people could do for us all!

Children really are the hope of the world. If you don't have young children, you can still help change the world by creating a shift in yourself. You are part of this world—if you shift, you will have helped move the world!

Your Subconscious Power

The second half of this book will focus on *you*—your subconscious power and how you can develop as a fulfilled person who lives in the present. In particular, you can overcome childhood challenges or perceived failures, and create incredible relationships from now on.

I will also discuss the basis of emotions and how to shift from living in a state of fear to living in a state of love. You will learn the power of goal setting and realize that **you can achieve anything you desire.**

I know your time is very valuable and I wish to thank you in advance for taking this opportunity to expand your awareness. Now, let's begin—and thank you again for joining me on this incredible journey.

2

Powerful And Positive Parenting

E rik Homburger Erikson was born in Germany in 1902. He conducted research on human development at Harvard, Yale, and the University of California at Berkeley. His theory of human development covers the entire life cycle from infancy through old age. He believed that the personality is not fixed and can change through middle and late adulthood. One of his biggest contributions to human development was the realization that each stage builds upon the foundation of the prior stage.

The Key First Years

Erikson's work showed that the first year of life is a vital period for the development of trust; between the ages of one and three years, the child needs to develop autonomy; and by the ages of three to five years, the child needs to develop initiative.

If a developmental stage is not achieved, each subsequent stage will be adversely affected. Like a building, if the foundation is not sturdy, the rest of the building will not be structurally sound. If mistrust predominates over trust in the first year of life, then shame, guilt, and inferiority may predominate over autonomy and initiative as development proceeds.

Mother-Child Bonding Sets The Stage For Future Development

The one individual who has the greatest predisposition for developing the fastest, most intimate bond with the infant is the mother. A lactating mother undergoes hormonal and neurochemical shifts that give her a heightened sense of awareness and supersensitivity to the environment.

Another example of this heightened sense of awareness is the premenstrual syndrome (PMS). This is not a curse from God, though many people think so. The hormonal and neurochemical shifts that women go through make them more sensitive to their emotions. Medical research has shown that serotonin levels in the blood decrease during this time. This decrease in serotonin has been linked to women's heightened sense of awareness and supersensitivity to the environment. This supersensitivity is needed for the survival of the species.

Early bonding between the baby and the primary caregiver is one of the most important events in the infant's life. This bonding will determine the ability of the growing child to develop self-trust as well as trust of the outside world. Many theories of human development point to this time as a key influence over the entire lifespan.

Understanding Babies: The Maternal Advantage

The newborn has limited means of communicating its needs. The infant cries, produces other noises, makes some movements, and emits some smells. With this information, the caregivers must know what to do. Heightened sensitivity and awareness helps the mother to know—on a more intuitive level—the needs of her infant.

> *"This nurturing role of the mother has been determined through natural evolution for the purpose of species survival."*
> —Prof. Mohammedreza Hojat, Thomas Jefferson School of Medicine

The mother's supersensitivity helps the development of the early bonding that is vital for all aspects of the infant's survival and growth.

The Caregiver's Key Role

Anyone, males or females, can attune themselves to a baby's needs if they spend the time as a caregiver.

How many times have you seen a babysitter fumble around trying to figure out why an infant is crying? Then the mother or father walks over and puts the infant on her or his shoulder—a loud belch is heard after a few pats, and the crying stops.

The interactions that unfold between the mother or primary caregiver and the infant must be consistent.

A baby needs the same caregivers, as much as possible, in the first 18 months.

The "Good-Enough" Or Healthy Caregiver

When an infant wets the diaper and cries, the "good-enough" or healthy caregiver quickly changes the diaper.

The "good-enough mother" was a term used by Donald Winnicott (a central figure in the British school of early relations theory) to describe a mother-infant relationship that meets the infant's needs in a healthy and consistent fashion. For instance, when an infant is hungry and begins to cry, the healthy caregiver feeds the infant.

Consistent and timely behavior produces in the infant a sense that discomfort will quickly resolve.

With a healthy caregiver, the infant begins to trust that the discomfort will be met quickly by extreme comfort to a point where the hunger becomes associated with a pleasurable response. For infants attended to by healthy caregivers, the world is experienced as a safe and com-

fortable place, and trust begins to form.

With this type of care-giving response, the discomfort brings less and less crying. Soon only a brief sound of discomfort is heard before the response is given.

The "Not-Good-Enough" Or Unhealthy Caregiver

Now let's look at the opposite extreme, a caregiver who may be depressed, or addicted to alcohol or another drug. The infant cries and receives no response. The infant continues to cry because of the discomfort and still receives no response because the primary caregiver is physically or emotionally absent.

This baby's understanding of the surrounding world is much different from that of an infant cared for by a healthy caregiver. The world does not make sense. Pain at times will last. There is no response to cries for relief and comfort. At other times, when the caregiver is sober and in a pleasant state, there is a quicker response.

RESPOND TO YOUR BABY

If you give a baby everything she appears to want, you are teaching her confidence that the world is a good place where her needs will be met....If you refuse to go to her, you...are teaching her to cry more and more and feel herself helpless, because, however many messages she sends, she cannot communicate with you.

—Penelope Leach, *The First Six Months: Getting Together with Your Baby*

There is no healthy conditioning taking place between the infant's world inside and the responses from the outside. The infant cannot trust its feelings, cannot trust that the discomfort will end. Despair can set in, and if the neglect is severe enough, the infant can become severely malnourished and fail to thrive.

The "Power" Of Neglect

The emotional bond in this early stage of life is so powerful that the instinct to survive can be stifled.

Dr. René Spitz studied orphaned infants after World War II. He noted that when the emotional bonding was lacking between the caregivers and the infants, the infants would stop taking in nutrition and become more susceptible to illness, and possibly die.

> *"Perhaps a child who is fussed over gets a feeling of destiny, he thinks he is in the world for something important and it gives him drive and confidence."*
>
> —Dr. Benjamin Spock

Another example of the lack of healthy emotional bonding is seen in children five years of age or older. These children exhibit a severe type of failure-to-thrive syndrome called psychosocial dwarfism. A chronically emotionally-deprived child does not grow or develop, even when nutrition is present. Endocrine changes result in decreased growth hormone and these children simply cease to grow.

Separation Depression

René Spitz also described a depression experienced by infants with normal attachments who were separated from their mothers for varying lengths of time. These infants became depressed, withdrawn, nonresponsive, and vulnerable to physical illness.

The infants recovered when their mother returned or surrogate mothering was provided within a short period of time.

Infants who survive a neglectful or inconsistent first 18 months of life will have severely impaired "object relations." What this means is that the relations the child has with people (objects) may be flawed. Some experts feel that the child may never recover from this deficit.

Infants who are neglected may also lack the stimulation to develop the intellectual capacity to function well in our society. I will discuss this in greater detail in the following chapters. They may also lack the emotional ability (recently called EQ for emotional quotient) to form healthy relationships. Both are vital in the overall functioning of the individual in society. The developmental groundwork for maximizing intellectual capacity and emotional stability are formed in the critical period before the age of 30 to 36 months of life.

We Can Improve Things

The United States' budget for 1997 earmarked $350 million more for the Head Start Program. Being a child and adolescent psychiatrist, I am overjoyed about the federal government increasing the funds to that population, but the timing is a critical mistake.

An Even Better Head Start

The Head Start program could have an immensely more powerful influence per dollar spent if the program shifted the start time to the sixth month of pregnancy! Currently, most Head Start programs begin when the child is three-and-a-half to four years of age.

A Shift In Timing

We must start supporting and stimulating the fetus, and nurturing the emotional bonding between the mother and her fetus. In one generation, we can make a drastic shift in the intellectual and emotional development of our children.

When this shift takes place, the impact of the increased intellect, along with the instilling of powerful character traits, will help change the multigenerational cycle of poverty, crime, and drugs that takes place in this country.

Unconditional Love

The interactions between the primary caregivers and the infant must be in terms of **unconditional positive regard**.

This means that the infant is accepted as all good. Drinks will be spilled, possessions may be scratched or broken, but the

"Well, I see she's reached the Age of Autonomy."

essence of your infant remains a miracle.

Life happens, and we cannot ask, "How could you do that to me?" to an 11-month-old who spilled a drink, or place guilt on a four-year-old when an illness hits on a planned evening out.

The message that needs to be given to the developing conscious and subconscious minds of infants is that they are accepted and loved.

As parents and other caregivers, we need to be tolerant, patient, and accepting of what life presents to us and deal with each situation with love in our hearts. We need to deal with the little spills as lessons in learning how to hold the glass, not as opportunities to ventilate anger and frustration.

Programming The Child's Subconscious

Think for a moment what happens in the mind of a child who is repeatedly scolded for accidents. The child is told he or she was wrong, or blamed out of our frustration.

Negative Programming

Here are just some examples of what repeatedly-scolded children feel and learn.

- They feel terrible.
- They feel like a failure.
- They feel angry.
- They begin to question their own abilities.
- They begin to shut down life's free flow of energy.
- They become insecure with their own judgement and decisions.
- They question who they are.
- They learn to respond in anger.
- They learn to yell at others.
- They learn that emotions are controlled by others, since what they did upset the parent.
- They learn to judge events as good or bad, right or wrong.
- They learn that life is not a flow but a regimented and structured thing that needs to be performed a certain way.
- They learn how to disrespect others.
- They learn to blame themselves.
- They learn to put themselves and others down.
- They feel they have disappointed their parents—their heroes.

Though these were not the desired messages, this is the process of learning when anger and frustration are the basis of parental interactions with their children.

Unresolved Adult Conflict Hurts Children

Many adults express frustration toward their infants because they haven't resolved deep conflicts in their own lives.

One easy way to measure the amount of unresolved conflict is to pay attention to how many times in a day you are upset, angry, anxious, disappointed, or frustrated. If you feel this way a majority of the time, then you are living in the shadow of past traumas or perceived failures of your life, and not in the present.

Don't "Let Off Steam" At Your Children

Life occurs in the here and now. When one lives in the past and is fixated away from the present, then negative emotions can abound. You'll tend to "ventilate" the built-up steam. You may become angry at work or at a friend. Or worse, you may take the opportunity to "discipline" your child to help release your "steam."

This is like a boiling pot on the stove. As the steam builds, the lid must be lifted off to let out the steam. This process repeats and repeats until the child, or now adolescent, may have severe behavior problems, be failing in school, turn to drugs (including alcohol), develops   poor or unhealthy peer relations, or becomes involved in crime. The child becomes what the parents feared he or she would become.

It's A Family Systems Problem

I have seen this scenario played out over and over in the children and adolescents I have treated.

Parents want me to "fix" the patient. But I spend as much time with the parents as I do with the patient, helping them to heal the traumas and perceived failures of their own pasts, and to begin interacting out of love and positive regard instead of fear, anger, and other negative emotions.

A mother came to a family clinic with severe relationship problems with her 14-year-old son. This was her third and youngest son. Her two older sons were placed in long-term residential treatment or group homes because of similar severe behavior problems when they were 14.

The Mother's Fears

The mother sought help this time at a family therapy clinic, a clinic that delved much deeper into the family system and not just that of the identified patient. As the therapy sessions unfolded, the mother's reaction to the problems seemed blown out of proportion and the focus shifted to her. She was asked, "What would happen if your son stayed at home and was not taken into a residential setting?" The mother broke down in tears and replied, "He will die."

She then elaborated on the history of her life. When she was about 11 years old, her mother died and she became the family caretaker. One night, her 15-year-old brother came down with a fever. She climbed in bed with him and put towels on his forehead late into the night trying to cool him off. When she awoke in the morning, he was dead. This 11-year-old girl never forgave herself and buried this fear of taking care of a 15-year-old boy deep in her subconscious mind.

Help The Parent First

When she became a mother, she could not accept the responsibility of caring for a 15-year-old boy. As each of her sons approached this age, "severe behavior problems arose" and her sons were removed from the home. Now that the truth was known, the therapist was able to help the mother heal her trauma and keep her 14-year-old son at home. This is a dramatic example of the fact that, as adults, we must all deal with our past issues or they will unfold in the relationships with our children and others in our lives.

The "Black Sheep"

Another way that parental frustrations can come out is in the myth that every family has a black sheep. This is a great example of how patients are "created" for us therapists. Parents who have not resolved their conflicts from their childhood or events in their past may select one child who is the farthest away from the ideal child they had in their minds. Then they let out their frustrations and anger on this child, and the child becomes whatever the parents have told the child he or she is.

Heal Yourself First

*The key to decreasing our need to ventilate the steam is to **turn off the stove so the steam never forms**.*

When we injure our knee playing basketball, do we go outside and yell at the ground, the hoop, or the ball for causing the pain? No, we nurture the sore knee. We put ice, then heat on it, we wrap it, and we permit it to heal.

The Blame Game Is A Lame Game

But when we get angry, we yell at who we think caused the anger (e.g., "He made me mad," "She makes me angry"), instead of nurturing ourselves and others. We blame the children, the boss, the job, the school, etc. We have learned to be great projectors instead of reflectors.

Important truth:
We need to reflect instead of project
when we are angry or frustrated.

Emotional pain is exactly the same as physical pain. The anger is inside of you. That is where we need to go for the healing to take place. We all have issues from childhood like not feeling listened to, not feeling supported or loved, or feeling scared or alone.

Our Childhood Issues

Any adult emotion that is strong and over-whelming for us has a high probability of being a childhood issue. Before the age of four to five years, our memories of events are not well formed because we do not have the language or mental capacity to store and recall on a conscious level details of experiences. What we do have is the stored memories of emotions.

Each day we may experience events in our adult life that trigger our childhood emotions. If we have not processed those traumas, or feelings of neglect or abandonment, we are living a limited existence held back by fears from our past experience.

Our anger is our issue, not our children's. Please do not teach children through anger or they will learn the above-stated negative messages.

"Anger is never without a reason, but seldom with a good one."
—Benjamin Franklin

The message is this:

We as parents need to interact with our children out of love and not out of fear, and use total positive regard instead of negative emotions.

The Right Messages For Children

When your children are acting up and need to be corrected, you must redirect, educate, and correct them immediately. I say immediately because you need them to associate the correction or redirection with the behavior that was improper. We are conditioning the child to know what to do and not do. If we wait one hour or two hours until we have let go of the anger, and then correct the child while they are playing quietly or behaving, they will be confused about the redirection. They will associate it with the current behavior.

Act With Love

We must redirect immediately with love in our hearts. So, when you feel the anger, place your hand on your chest, over your sternum or heart. Next, breathe as if the breath is flowing directly into your hand, circling around your heart, and flowing out of your mouth. Imagine a half circle of breath flowing into your hand and out of your mouth. Then focus on the joy, excitement, and love you felt when you held your baby for the first time, or experienced your first kiss, or embraced a lover. Fill yourself with this feeling.

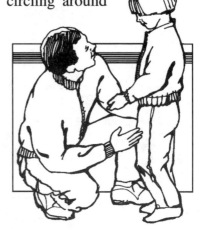

Now come back to the moment and redirect your child out of love. Do not turn into a marshmallow, and say, "That's okay Joey" etc. Love is powerful, disciplined, yet accepting and nonjudgmental. Your child will feel the love and want to listen and learn. If we react out of anger, they feel the anger and turn off. They will learn only how to react in anger and the lesson is lost.

The other powerful conditioning that is taking place is that you will soon be immediately able to interact with your child and anyone else through love. By doing this, you will always produce the desired result.

The Results Of Interacting Through Love

The message they will learn will be incredible.

- I am loved.
- Everything is a learning experience.
- I can flow with life and I will be supported and loved.
- I am wonderful.
- I am a gift to this world.
- I deserve to be treated with respect.
- Life is about being happy and loving.
- Happiness comes from inside myself.
- I am responsible for my emotions.
- I am confident.
- I can live and achieve out of love and happiness, instead of the illusion that I need to achieve to obtain happiness and love.
- I can forgive and tolerate the behavior of others.
- I can see that there is always a positive side to every event that occurs.
- Even when I am feeling great pain, I can still

respond with love and happiness.

- I will treat others with respect.

These are the messages that our children need to hear and incorporate into their conscious and subconscious minds. (I'll discuss more about your mind in the second half of the book.)

You can also build a positive attitude and unconditional positive regard in your children. Children have the desire to be seen as "the best child" or have the love of their parents above their brothers or sisters (siblings).

Sibling Rivalry

These days we're all familiar with the term sibling rivalry. Every time a child's sibling does something wrong, the child tells Mommy or Daddy because they know Mommy or Daddy will punish the bad behavior. The child also can feel that he or she is helping Mommy and Daddy and gaining favor in their eyes.

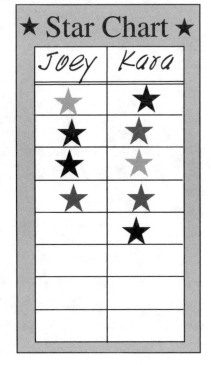

Here's how to turn negative tattling around. When you reward positive behavior and positive feedback, you will direct your children to begin looking at the positive actions of their siblings. They will start to learn to focus on the positive.

Design a reward system with a "gold star" chart or some other method that rewards good comments about siblings. If one child, for example, tells you "Joey made his bed, Mom," reward both the child who told you and Joey. Celebrate when the star charts or other reward devices are full or completed. Don't celebrate by giving candy or a toy. Instead, take your child to the park or a movie so you can enjoy the celebration together.

Just think how much better you will feel when your children are telling you all the great things each of them did through the day.

Love Is Powerful

We must balance discipline and structure with freedom and acceptance. Remember, the extreme of all love and acceptance without structure and discipline can create children and teens with emotional problems. The extreme of all structure and discipline without love and acceptance can do the same.

Parenting must be out of the emotion and power of love. If we are doing this, we are on the right path.

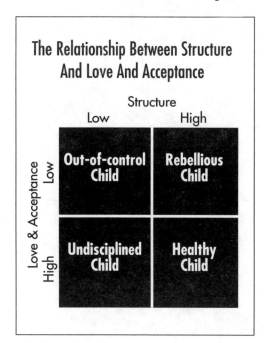

The Relationship Between Structure And Love And Acceptance

	Structure	
	Low	High
Love & Acceptance — Low	Out-of-control Child	Rebellious Child
Love & Acceptance — High	Undisciplined Child	Healthy Child

3

Early Stimulation Of Your Child

T o better understand the powerful way that early stimulation provides a strong foundation for your child, let's look at Nature and the stimulation that is provided to the developing fetus.

The Sense Of Hearing

Hearing is the most developed sense at birth because the fetus can hear through the liquid environment in the womb.

We, and Nature, do not limit the amount of sound being heard by the infant to what is understood. The infant hears many interesting sounds, sounds we wouldn't normally think about. These include rushing blood, stomach sounds, the heart beating, breathing, as well as sounds from the outside environment. Though the infant cannot understand these sounds, they are present and necessary for the complex sense of hearing to develop.

Singing In the Brain

Researchers at the University of Konstanz in Germany reported that music rewires brain cell connections. The brains of nine string players were examined with MRI (magnetic resonance imaging). The amount of cortex (brain matter) dedicated to the thumb and fifth finger of the left hand—the digits used in fingering the stringed instrument—was significantly greater in the musicians as compared to those who did not play.

It is important to note that it was **the age when they started to play** a musical instrument that determined the cortical mapping, not the hours spent playing. They found that the earlier the exposure to the instrument, the more brain matter was dedicated to playing it.

Music For The Brain

Research on children who received systematic prenatal stimulation through music finds that these children show higher levels of attention and vocalization than children who are exposed to music later. Listening to music also increases intelligence and encourages discipline, attention, fluency, and self-reliance. Early exposure to music not only increases musical aptitude but components of other areas of giftedness.

—Emily P. Carey, *Roeper Review*

Music Improves Spatial Ability

Gordon Shaw and Frances Rauscher at the University of California, Irvine, studied the power of music in three- to five-year-old preschoolers. Nineteen preschoolers received weekly keyboard lessons and sang daily in chorus. Another 15 preschoolers were not exposed to the music training. After eight months the musical group demonstrated "dramatically improved spatial reasoning."

"Music is a more potent instrument than any other for education."

—Plato

They scored as much as 80% higher in spatial intelligence than the playmates who did not receive music lessons. Spatial intelligence was measured by working mazes, puzzles, drawing geometric figures, and copying patterns of two-color blocks. Spatial intelligence is our ability to visualize or conceptualize the world. This skill later translates into areas such as complex math, problem solving, and engineering. One conclusion by Gordon Shaw was, "Early music training can enhance a child's ability to reason."

Music Enhances Science Ability

Pauline Einstein, the mother of Albert Einstein, was a great lover of music. Before the age of six, Albert began to play the violin and would do so on a daily basis to calm himself. Though he never became a great violinist, we now know what else he may have been developing as he played.

Schools on average have only one music teacher for every 500 children.
—National Commission on Music Education

There is no question that music develops in the brain the connections needed for higher forms of thinking.

In a survey of science achievement in eighth

and ninth graders, Hungary ranked first and the U.S. 14th out of 17 nations. Hungary, as you may have guessed, has one of the most rigorous school music programs in the world, with instruction starting at the kindergarten level.

Kinesthetic Stimulation

Another type of stimulation that happens naturally in the womb is from movement by the mother and the baby.

As the mother goes about her business during the day, walking and making other movements, the fetus moves in the womb. The baby can also move in the womb to produce kinesthetic feedback. For instance, you may have seen ultrasound pictures of babies sucking their thumbs in the womb.

In addition to incidental movements communicating to the baby, you can deliberately stimulate the baby this way. For instance, I know of one father who would tap on the mother's abdomen be-

"Children's training in music as introducing rhythm and harmony into their souls and having a socializing influence; for the whole life of man stands in need of rhythm and harmony... The ultimate end of all eduation is insight into the harmonious order (Cosmos) of the whole world."
—Plato, *The Republic of Plato*

The Power Of Touch

Tactile stimulation is also important. Preterm children who receive systematically applied tactile stimulation after they are born score significantly higher on intelligence and achievement tests at age seven. It is very likely that tactile stimulation also enhances intelligence for normal-term children.

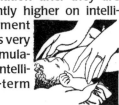

– E.N. Adamson-Macedo et al., *Journal of Reproductive and Infant Psychology*

fore talking to the fetus. Music can also be chosen to set up rhythms that are transmitted to the baby.

Use Tools

After the baby is born, you can use blocks and other objects to help develop the spatial and kinesthetic senses. For instance, Montessori and Waldorf schools use a series of exercises involving different shapes, textures, and weights. They may give children a set of blocks that differs in size, color, or texture. The variations help train the children's perceptions and stimulate them with the variety.

Neuroscientist William Greenough, at the University of Illinois, studied the brain development of rats in different physically stimulating environments. One group of rats was "couch potatoes" and did nothing. A second group exercised on an automatic treadmill. The third group of rats was set loose in an obstacle course that required them to perform numerous acrobatic feats.

Only 36% of the schoolchildren today are required to participate in daily physical education. (*Newsweek*, February 19, 1996)

The third group of rats were found to have "an enormous amount of gray matter" (brain cells) as compared to the first sedentary group.

Stimulating Your Fetus

Imagine counting numbers, performing addition, subtraction, and other math problems, for the benefit of the fetus, even though they cannot comprehend what they are hearing. What this stimulation will do is to develop that part of their brain that will, in the future, be called upon to comprehend these types of problems.

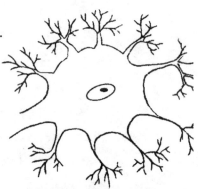

A NEURON or BRAIN CELL with branched extensions called DENDRITES. Dendrites conduct impulses from adjacent cells.

With this stimulation, the neurons will *maximally* form connections in the areas needed to comprehend the most complex verbally-described problems that may be encountered.

If understimulated, then simpler forms of math or problem solving may be very difficult. This is exactly what is happening in some poorer socioeconomic groups.

Don't Overstimulate

In studies of infant response, overstimulation can easily scare and turn off a baby's awareness. Holding a baby close to one's face and excitedly and rapidly talking without a break can be a frightening thing to a two-month-old.

Provide stimulation in a soft, soothing, and loving voice. Talk to your babies with the understanding that they will have no idea what you are saying—they may show more attentiveness to your nose or eyes than any words.

The human brain adds an astonishing 350,000 neurons per minute during the first six months of pregnancy. That is almost 6,000 brain cells per second. Now is the time for us to start directing the next miraculous process (massive dendritic formation) with reasonable and loving fetal stimulation.   - John M. Mike, MD

Start Gently

This is fine. Remember that you are stimulating the dendritic development of the brain, not through the infant's understanding but through the massive intellectual potential the human brain possesses. We are not doing this to see some light of awareness of our words, but the infant will recognize our voice and, soon, our face.

Stimulation must be balanced with rest and sleep. Starting as early as the sixth month of pregnancy, or any time you are inspired by love, talk to the fetus with your hand placed over the womb.

The emotion behind the voice must be in a state of love. We know that the power of love is essential for development. Healthy growth not only needs nutrients, but also emotional bonding. If a loving bond is not formed between the infant and the mother, or the primary caregiver, a high percentage of these infants will have developmental or emotional delays.

Mothers' Emotions Affect Babies

The scientific literature is full of studies showing that stress can lower the immune system's response, making us more susceptible to infections. Also, suppressed anger has been found to be the number one risk factor for heart attacks in those with a Type A personality.

A mother's emotional state can affect the baby. For instance, a mother's anger releases hormones and other chemicals that enter into the mother's bloodstream and through the umbilical cord into the bloodstream of the fetus.

Numerous studies have found that the incidence of psychiatric illness in children rises due to the increased stress in the mother's life during the pregnancy. One such study in Europe found that the loss of the fathers during the pregnancy, through accidents or other factors, led to a six-fold increase in the development of schizophrenia in the group of children studied when compared to the control population. The researchers speculated that the higher rates of schizophrenia were caused by mothers releasing increased levels of hormones, possibly cortisol, during periods of stress. These hormones could change the neuronal migration in the developing brain, making these children more susceptible to developing schizophrenia.

Thinking about how to help your baby develop optimally will also help you. The process of being and living in a state of love and caring makes our lives full and helps us become more connected to our friends, family, and ourselves. This balanced state helps us live healthier lives.

Visual Stimulation

The glory of vision doesn't happen all at once for the baby. Once the infant is born, light strikes the infant's eyes. Newborns can only see a very small fraction of what they are shown—and they comprehend less than that.

We, and Nature, stimulate the infant well beyond the infant's ability to understand that stimulation. Understanding grows over time because the dendritic formation in the brain continues to occur, and the baby begins to respond to the stimulation. (See the next chapter for a discussion of brain development.)

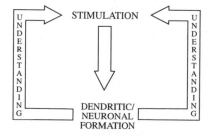

A cyclic process is set up where the stimulation leads to dendritic formation and possibly new neuronal formation. This in turn helps the infant to understand the very stimulation that is applied. The stimulation creates the instrument for its own interpretation.

Language Stimulation

By the first year of life, babies have already begun to **lose** the ability to discriminate sounds not in their native language. Patricia Kuhl of the University of Washington, using electrical measurements that identified neurons responding to different sounds, found that "infants have lost the ability to discriminate sounds that are not significant in their language, and their babbling has acquired the sound of their language."

Stimulate Vocabulary

The more words a child hears, the faster and more vast a vocabulary they will possess. Dr. Janellen Huttenlocher of the University of Chicago found that infants whose mothers spoke frequently to them had a vocabulary of 131 more words than infants of less verbally involved mothers. At 24 months the difference increased to 295 words.

In a review of the literature, researchers at the University of Leiden's Center for Child and Family Studies have found the quality of attachment between the infant and parent is strongly associated with the infant's language development.

This attachment is also significantly associated with cognitive development as assessed by IQ and DQ (development quotient). They note that secure parents may be better teachers and secure children may be better motivated students.

Stimulate Baby Plus Yourself

Language, music, and movement are all a part of fetal and infant stimulation.

Talk to your developing baby about all areas of learning—math, English, literature, history, geography, astronomy, music, art, science, philosophy, sociology, psychology—or any other areas you are inspired to teach. The different words and sounds are needed to create the massive dendritic formation the brain is capable of forming.

Young babies won't be able to tell the difference between the subjects you cover. But the variety will also keep you interested and learning.

Play classical and New Age music for your child during fetal development and after birth.

In the womb, the fetus is stimulated through the movements of the mother. After your child is born, stimulate your infant with physical movement by gently moving your infant's arms and legs.

Build Character

We must work on the character principles with our children. Intellect without character is like a house without supports. Knowledge provides the building blocks, but character provides the underlying support.

Character principles include honesty, courage, discipline, empathy, compassion, passion, commitment, sharing, caring, integrity, playfulness and, most importantly, love.

In our Western culture

"Character is higher than intellect."
—Ralph Waldo Emerson

we have become great doers and builders, but we
have often forgotten how to live.

Character Unifies

All of the character principles described have
been studied throughout human history at different
times, but never so intensely as in this last century.
These principles are a standard operating system for
the most successful and emotionally balanced people
in this world. You can achieve wealth without them.
But you can never happily achieve it, nor once you
have achieved it, live in a state of happiness.

Unity And Flow

Our body, minds, and spirits must be unified to
live in a state of wholeness and oneness in order to
flow through the events of life rather than struggle
against them. That oneness can only occur if we
live by these character principles.

Your "flow" is easily disrupted when you break
from these principles. The divergence from these
principles can be felt
emotionally and physi-
cally. It is vital that you
add the character prin-
ciples to your early
stimulation program.

Do not begin the
stimulation process out of
anxiety. Don't worry that

Go With The Flow

Dr. Mihaly Csikszentmihalyi at the University of Chicago conducted a ground-
breaking study on the nature of optimal
experience, or what he calls "flow." A flow
state is that time when a person is pursuing
goals that stretch his or her abilities. "The
best moments usually occur when a person's
body or mind is stretched to its limits in a
voluntary effort to accomplish something
difficult and worthwhile."

you are not doing it right, or how long to do it, or exactly what material to cover. Do not feel guilty because you believe you are not covering enough material. Just speak to your child out of love and end any negative thoughts.

The Power Of Thoughts

Our thoughts are real. They have power and they exist in the world. The fetus can feel them, sense them, and they will affect the developing infant and child.

When we stimulate the fetus, it is vital that it be in the state of love, and that we have faith that what we are doing is just perfect. If we do it with confidence and love in our hearts, then it *is* just perfect.

Love Is Perfect

Remember there is no single right way. There is always a balance between body, mind, and spirit. The fetus must have quiet, peaceful, and restful times as well as times for stimulation and focus.

In addition to direct stimulation of your baby by talking about a particular subject, communication and bonding can occur

throughout the day when you feel
the internal desire and are inspired
to do so.

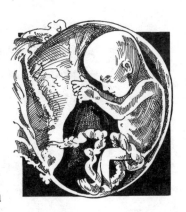

> *Relate to your baby*
> *through, love, commitment,*
> *and peace.*

The length of time of "stimulation sessions" will be something you
will have to gauge by your infant's
response. Direct stimulation can occur one hour a day during the
sixth month and then one-and-a-half to two hours a day during
the seventh, eighth, and ninth months. Talk, read, or play a tape
for approximately 20 minutes at a time during the sixth month.
Then increase up to 30-minute sessions as you approach the
ninth month.

Research in the area of fetal stimulation is in the beginning
stage. There is a growing body of knowledge on the impact of
stimulation, but the details and types of stimulation are not well
defined. The above is a common sense guideline that permits
both stimulation and necessary periods of rest and relaxation.

Maintain Potential

At conception, we are pure unlimited potential! Development
starts to be affected by the thoughts of the mother and those
around her. If the thoughts are severely negative, there can be an
incredible disruption in normal development. I have already
discussed the study that found a six-fold increase in schizophrenia in the children whose mothers lost their husbands during the
pregnancy.

The food the mother eats affects the development of the fetus. Similarly, repetitive thoughts you have will impact the development of the fetus.

There are numerous studies demonstrating the affects that diet and habits, such as drinking and smoking, have on the developing fetus. We know that our thoughts affect our own bodies, and we are just beginning to understand the effects of our thoughts on the developing fetus.

Faith Heals

The cover story of *Time* magazine (June 24, 1996) is about the power of faith in healing. "A 1995 study at Dartmouth-Hitchcock Medical Center found that one of the best predictors of survival among 232 heart surgery patients was the degree to which patients said they drew comfort and strength from religious faith. Those who did not had more than three times the death rate than those who did."

Other results noted in the faithful were:
- lower blood pressure
- reduced risk of dying of coronary artery disease, and
- less risk of developing depression and anxiety-related illness.

"Anywhere from 60% to 90% of visits to doctors are in the mind-body, stress-related realm," asserts Dr. Herbert Benson, president of the Mind/Body Medical Institute of Boston's Deaconess Hospital and Harvard Medical School.

The Power of Prayer

There are currently over 350 research papers on the subject of the power of prayer and faith in the healing process. Larry Dossey, MD, has noted the findings of many scientific papers alluding to the power of prayer.

One such paper was designed by cardiologist Randolph Byrd, MD. Over a 10-month period, a computer program randomly assigned 393 patients admitted to the coronary care unit at San Francisco General Hospital to either a prayed-for group or to a group that was not remembered in prayer. It was a randomized double-blind experiment in which neither the patients, nurses, or doctors knew which group the patients were in. The prayer groups were given the first names of their patients as well as a brief description of their diagnosis and condition. They were asked to pray each day. Each patient had 5–7 people praying for him or her.

The results showed that the prayed-for patients differed in several ways:

- They were five times less likely to require antibiotics.
- They were three times less likely to develop pulmonary edema (fluid in the lungs).
- None of the prayed-for group required endotracheal intubation (in which an artificial airway is inserted in the throat and attached to a mechanical ventilator). Twelve in the group not remembered in prayer required mechanical ventilation.
- Fewer patients in the prayed-for group died (although this difference was not statistically significant).

Thoughts Affect The World

Dr. Dossey notes many flaws in the study, including a possibility that the group not remembered in prayer may have prayed for themselves or had family members who prayed for them. He then looked at nonhuman studies. These studies researched the effects of conscious intent or prayer on fungi, yeast, or bacteria. The following are some of the results.

- Ten subjects tried to inhibit the growth of fungus cultures through conscious intent by concentrating on them for 15 minutes from a distance of approximately 15 yards. Of a total of 194 culture dishes, 151 showed retarded growth.

- In a replication of this study, one group of subjects demonstrated the same effect (inhibiting the growth of the fungus) in 16 out of 16 trials, while stationed from one to 15 miles away from the cultures.

- 160 subjects, not known to have healing abilities, were able to both impede and stimulate the growth of cultures of bacteria.

The point is, if praying to God, or a cosmic consciousness, can create a shift in yourself or another human being whom you don't know, just think how powerful your thoughts are on the development of your fetus. When pregnant, be mindful of your thoughts and live in a state of peace, harmony, and love as much as possible. Nothing is more important to the developing fetus than to have an environment of healthy nutrients *and* thoughts.

In Conclusion

The weight of a newborn's brain is approximately 350 grams. It will grow to the adult weight of 1450 grams. Most of the weight gain is due to dendritic formation.

Newborn
brain
350 grams

Remember, stimulation of your children should start by the sixth month of pregnancy. Emotional bonding can start taking place the moment after conception.

The material you use for stimulation should be broad in its presentation and must include character principles.

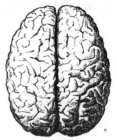

The emotions that occur in pregnant women affect their children's development. The number one emotion that should be experienced by the pregnant women is love.

Adult brain
1450 grams

4

Your Brain's Potential

Knowledge about the human brain is exploding as more funds are devoted to this area of research. Now is the time to greatly increase the intellectual capacity of the very organ we are so passionately trying to understand.

Your Child's Brain

What begins after conception is a process of magnificent cell division, growth, maturation, and specialization. The first signs of the human brain appear around the **16th day**. Development continues at such a torrid pace that, by the end of the sixth month, the fetus has essentially all the neurons that will ever be present.

Brain Structure

Neurons are the cells of the brain that transfer information through chemical and electrical communication. Dendrites are the connections between the neurons which permit them to communicate.

By the sixth month essentially of all the neurons are in place and the fetus will not be receiving many more. As the neurons are stimulated, "branches" (dendrites) form. Dendritic connections between neurons continue to evolve as more and more information is processed.

I say that *essentially* all neurons are present by six months because research on brain cells has shown that the brain cells of infants may in fact reproduce if stimulated by a neuron growth hormone. This finding transcends the old belief that brain cells do not reproduce.

Branching Neurons

Imagine that the neurons are the tree trunks and the dendrites are the branches. The leaves are the synaptic clefts or communication zones between neurons.

Just as a tree grows when we add water, nutrients, and sunlight, the connections within the brain grow when they receive stimulation.

What would happen if we were to deprive a tree of the needed nutrients or sunshine? It would never reach its maximal potential. Though the tree can survive, the trunk would not be as thick, the branches would not be as full, and the leaves would be less abundant and less green.

Dendrites

Stimulate Connections

In order for us to reach our maximum intellectual potential, our brains must be stimulated

Synapse

NEURONS

to form the vital connections between neurons.

Your intelligence is not based on the size of your brain, but on the number of connections between the parts of your brain. To use a computer metaphor, it's not the number of chips in your brain, but how they are wired together.

These connections permit communication to take place between different parts of our brain. The connections are vital for us to comprehend incoming stimuli from different parts of our body and our external world.

A Critical Period For Early Stimulation

Studies with kittens have shown that if you cover a newborn kitten's eyes after birth and remove the covers nine months later, the kitten will be blind.

Even though the kitten has normal eyes and a normal brain, the dendritic connections between the optic nerve and critical areas of the brain have not formed. The sense of sight is lost. This is also true of human babies.

The other important point is that once the **critical period** for this development has passed, no matter how much stimulation is provided, sight cannot be restored.

The critical period has also been demonstrated with goslings. Goslings will accept as their mother, and follow, the first moving object they see after birth. Konrad Lorenz, the Nobel prize winning ethologist, described his experience as the first object in the sight of goslings after birth. He was "imprinted" in the goslings minds as being their mother and they devoutly followed him around.

Areas Of The Brain

The brain has been extensively mapped out over the past 50 years. When a person has a stroke and loses part of his or her normal functioning, a neurologist can exam the patient, note the deficit, and predict where the stroke occurred in the brain.

For instance, if a person were to have a stroke in Broca's area, the ability to produce speech would be lost, but the comprehension of language would remain intact. If a stroke occurred in Wernicke's area, speech would be intact but the words would not be in proper order or syntax and make no sense.

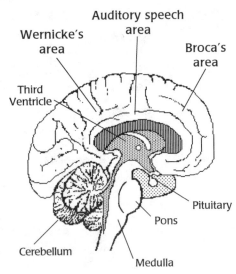

This understanding of the nature of the brain has brought forth new concepts of human brain development and function.

Stimulating Children's Brains

All this leads to the idea that as an infant grows and develops, the stimulation that is provided helps to develop the specific area of the brain needed to process that very stimulation.

Nature's Wonderful System

Simply stated, this means that sound helps develop the sense of hearing, and light and visual stimuli help develop the sense of sight. If we want to improve language development, we stimulate those areas of the brain involved in language processing. Similarly, math stimulation helps develop those areas of the brain involved in that function, as well as music, art, and so on.

> *The first three years of life is the critical period for dendritic formation. Without the proper amount of stimulation during this critical period, massive dendritic formation does not occur. This means that the particular areas of the brain that will process math, English, and science, for example, have not made the maximum number of connections between neurons.*

Disadvantaged Children

When understimulated children enter school, they will have a more difficult time comprehending and learning.

Once a child starts to fall behind, frustration builds. Even when this inability to perform is not the child's fault, the child is blamed for his or her actions. This then leads to self-criticism, low self-esteem, and increased frustration. These may then lead to behavioral difficulties.

Most often, these disadvantaged children are passed through the early grades. Some are transferred to less challenging classes, or put into classes with other behaviorally or emotionally disturbed children. This process creates a sense of failure, inferiority, and impairment.

If this continues through the teenage years, it can lead to further self- and societal-harming beliefs and behaviors. The cost to society, and more importantly to the developing human being, is astronomical.

Maximizing Our Potential

If we promote increased stimulation from the sixth month of pregnancy to three years old, we can make a dramatic shift in the average IQ functioning in the range of 20 to 40 points. This would translate to our children's average IQ shifting from 100 to between 120 and 140. By giving children the brain power that is needed to function in this complex world, they can begin the process of realizing their full potential.

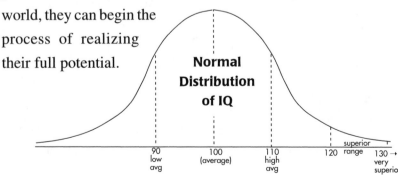

Normal Distribution of IQ

| | | | | superior range | |
| 90 low avg | 100 (average) | 110 high avg | 120 | 130 → very superior |

Helping Everyone

In our current system, people of lower socio-economic status tend on average to live in environments that stimulate children less. And these children who are stimulated less tend to have lower IQs.

It is counterproductive to focus on what test scores are now. Instead, we can increase *all* children's stimulation which will improve their brain power and their circumstances. We'll then be improving the total human resource for all of us!

Remember the words of Benjamin Franklin, "An ounce of prevention is worth a pound of cure."

This is an incredible understatement in terms of the human potential that is lost from the lack of early brain stimulation. A new generation of brighter and emotionally connected children could create incredible wonders for this world and humankind.

Reading For Stimulation

In my work in child psychiatry, I have seen numerous cases of the power of early stimulation. These were children stimulated by a parent or parents since birth, or starting during the pregnancy.

These children had IQs of 140 or greater and were in advanced classes or gifted programs. This has sometimes occurred as a secondary result of the parents reading to a sibling who was older but in the same room as the newborn.

For instance, I just performed an evaluation of a nine-year-old girl whose grades are starting to deteriorate because of family difficulties. When discussing early development, the father stated that he and his wife would read to their two-and-a-half year old and this child because they were in the same room. They would just read to them both side by side. This started when the girl was just a few weeks old.

The nine-year-old attends one of the most advanced programs in the state of Florida. She is in the Magnet Program— Center for Advanced International Studies. Her IQ is over 140! Her great potential will be permitted to unfold after dealing with the current family challenge.

In Conclusion

We're beginning to understand the many complexities of the human brain. It is widely accepted that we currently use only a small part of our potential brain power.

To maximize the incredible potential of your child, stimulation should start by the sixth month of pregnancy. Massive dendritic formation occurs in the first 36 months of life. Emotional stability plays a vital role in allowing our children and ourselves to tap into this incredible potential.

5

The Mind

The conscious mind is defined as that which we are aware of or can readily retrieve through memory. The subconscious mind is everything else.

Using the analogy of an iceberg, our conscious mind can be understood as the small part of the iceberg that is above water, that everyone can see. The subconscious mind is the much larger and vaster part of the iceberg submerged under the water that cannot readily be seen.

Our deepest conflicts reside in the deepest part of the iceberg and are the most difficult to uncover. Also, the iceberg is constantly changing and melting, its water merging with the vast ocean, just as our minds are constantly merging with the greater mind or universal consciousness.

We have images of who and what we are in our subconscious mind. Within this subconscious realm is a belief system of how we deserve to be treated and what life is about.

When an iceberg floats through the ocean, whichever direction the base is traveling, the tip will follow. This also applies to us.

The image we have in our subconscious minds will motivate and guide our conscious choices to fulfill that image.

A Model Of The Mind And Body

We think in terms of pictures. When I ask you to think of your car or your home, you immediately form a picture in your conscious mind.

In discussing the subconscious mind, a model can help us understand the concept. The series of drawings in this section were inspired by Bob Proctor, CEO of LifeSuccess Institute. These have been the most useful illustrations I have ever seen on this subject. They will also give us a chance to gain a deeper understanding of this powerful force that guides our lives.

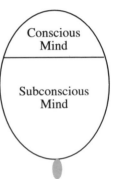

This illustration depicts the subconscious mind, the conscious mind, and the body. The conscious mind is the seat of our freewill, judgments, our perceptions of the world, and memory.

Imagine for a moment you are sitting on a beach on a colorful beach towel. You are wearing sunglasses and covered in suntan lotion. The waves are crashing in, the sun is shining, and you are reading this book. Take a few moments, close your eyes and imagine. As you can see, your imagination

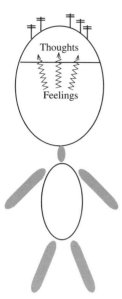

is also a part of your conscious mind.

The ability to be intuitive also lies in the conscious mind. Part of how the conscious mind, and your intuition, functions is through the five senses of vision, hearing, taste, touch, and smell which are depicted by the small antenna on the conscious mind.

The Subconscious Mind

The subconscious mind is expressed through *consistent* dreams, feelings, and actions. It is through these expressions that we are able to become aware of the images we have in our subconscious.

It is these expressions that a patient in therapy discusses, and is guided to gain conscious awareness of their meaning. As I have previously explained, the subconscious is the guiding force of our lives.

The body is the housing, the manifestation, and instrument of the mind. The body does not create; it manifests and is directed by the mind.

The images which we consistently create in our conscious mind implant in our subconscious mind. Whether we focus on the goals and mission of our lives or think about past failures and challenges, they implant into the subconscious.

We are directed in our feelings and actions by

our subconscious images. Our actions in turn create the results we have in our lives. This is why we need to actively focus on our goals and desires to implant those images in our subconscious.

Redesign Your Own Subconscious

Our subconscious minds were not designed by us but by all those around us while we were growing up. Babies are like sponges with, literally, pure subconscious minds. The conscious mind (ego) has not formed yet and they are totally accepting of what they perceive and are told.

Santa Claus is definitely accepted if children are told he exists. There is no judgment of the information. This is why babies and young children up to approximately age six can learn any subject we teach them, from languages to music. Remember, the earlier, the easier. For the young, information goes directly into the subconscious mind. As the ego or conscious mind forms, this process slows.

Programming The Subconscious

When you watch a two-year-old having a temper tantrum, you can tell that his entire body is involved in the emotional expression of the subconscious, and partial conscious mind. If repeated often enough, messages and associated feelings like "you are bad," "you can't do that," "that is impossible," "you are stupid," or "this colored, sweetened cereal makes you happy" all become implanted in body feelings and the subconscious mind.

As stated previously, the ability to remember details of events is not well developed before four to five years old. The conscious mind, language, and conscious memory are not fully in place. But memories of feelings are retained in the subconscious and experienced on a daily basis as they percolate into the conscious mind.

The Subconscious Starts Early

I believe the subconscious is present even before birth and has already begun the process of implanting information. The connection to the universal conscious mind is also in place before birth.

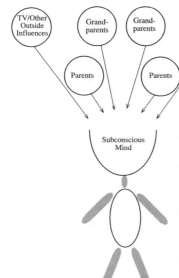

Infants and young children learn on a subconscious level. They therefore are incredible retainers of new information. Their subconscious image of who they are and what life is about is being formed not by them but by those influences around them.

We as adults can direct the subconscious influences on our feelings and actions by implanting powerful images in our conscious mind on a consistent basis. (This will be covered in great depth in the chapter on "Reprogramming the Subconscious Mind.")

The Subconscious Mind Directs

Clearly understood examples of the power of the subconscious are seen by counselors, psychologists, and psychiatrists throughout the world.

For example, many adults who were abused as children enter into abusive relationships. Abused as children, they may develop the subconscious belief that they deserve to be abused. They feel that they deserve to be treated poorly, that they don't merit respect, and that their feelings and thoughts do not matter.

The Subconscious Victim

If you ask people in abusive relationships if these are the types of relationships they want, or if this is how they wish to be treated, most would reply no.

The choice is made because their subconscious self-image proclaims, "I am a victim" and "I do not matter." This negative image guides their conscious choices. The person with whom they enter into a relationship is the one who fulfills this subconscious image and turns out to be an abuser.

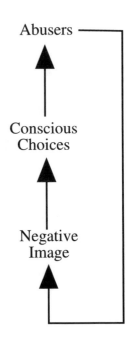

Abusers

Conscious Choices

Negative Image

The abuse often takes place over many years. Finally, after numerous family members, counselors, therapists, and friends provide enough support, the "victim" decides to leave the abusive relationship. However, if the subconscious self-image has not shifted through a process of reprogramming, the next person with whom he or she chooses to have a relationship will also likely be abusive—and the cycle repeats itself.

Rejecting Healthy Relationships

When an individual who is kind, caring, and sensitive wants to form a relationship with this abused person (whom I will call Sally), Sally often feels "I just don't love him" or "There is no spark." One clear reason for Sally's lack of passion for an emotionally healthy person is that her subconscious image is not being fulfilled. In fact, just the opposite is being triggered.

For Sally, a healthy relationship actually causes discomfort and can even make Sally physically ill. Mr. Sensitive sincerely wants to know how Sally is feeling, shows respect towards her, and listens to what she has to say. This treatment is foreign to Sally's subconscious image and produces discomfort. For this reason, people can, and do, "choose" abusive relationships over healthy ones.

It's easy to identify people who have an unhealthy subconscious image. These are the people always complaining about how they and others are treated unfairly or cruelly. They project anger onto everyone and everything with statements like, "He/she makes me furious," "I hate" this or that, etc. They tend to focus on the negative side of life's situations.

Overcoming Challenges

Not everyone who is abused forms negative images. All we need is one person, a teacher, a coach, a family member, including our own internal voice, to tell us we are loved, deserve to be treated with respect, and deserve to be happy. This may be all that we need to create a healthy subconscious image.

The wonderful thing is that we can shift our subconscious image to be very powerful and positive.

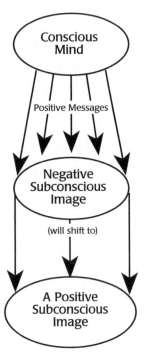

We are the masters of our destiny through the reprogramming of our subconscious minds. (More on this in Chapter 8.)

Your Subconscious Image

To better understand your own subconscious image, you can look at the decisions you've made in your life, the people who are around you, and what thoughts you carry throughout each day. If you have thoughts of guilt or shame, wish harm to others because they have hurt you, or harbor ill will toward anyone, know that these are the thoughts of your subconscious mind about yourself.

Every strong emotion, or frequent thought you have about another person is a thought you have about yourself.

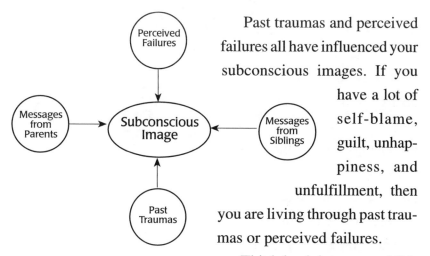

Past traumas and perceived failures all have influenced your subconscious images. If you have a lot of self-blame, guilt, unhappiness, and unfulfillment, then you are living through past traumas or perceived failures.

Think back into your childhood. Discuss your past with your parents if they are still alive, or your brothers and sisters. Think about the messages you were given and how your subconscious mind was influenced.

In the end, most of us have to forgive our parents and let go. There is no blame and the forgiveness is for our own sake.

Perceptions Of Reality

Disturbances in our past that upset us or caused frustration or disappointment often are not even based in reality, but on our perceptions of reality as children. When a child is four or five years old, a divorce or the birth of a sibling can be very painful. It's hard to say how a specific child may interpret a given event. Children at different stages of development give the same event different meanings.

You Make The World Go Round

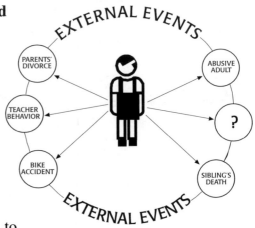

Four- and five-year-olds think in an egocentric manner—they believe they are the cause of everything around them. So if there is a divorce, what enters a child's mind is, "I am to blame for my parents problems" or "I am the reason mommy or daddy left." Even though the thought is not reality, this perception of reality can create a certain subconscious image or picture.

Life events do not have any meaning except the meaning that we give them. The application of meaning to an event becomes your conscious and subconscious reality.

For example, the death of a sibling can be very powerful in creating a subconscious image of self-blame or guilt.

If a child has had jealous feelings towards a sibling and at times wished his sibling dead, then the actual death is likely to make the child feel responsible for the sibling's death. It's clearly not the child's fault—no one is to blame—but the inter-pretation and the image that is created in the sub-conscious mind will influence the child's entire life.

Positive Thoughts Work

Basically, what it comes down to is how much time during the day do you spend on negative thoughts? The more time spent on negative thoughts, the more reprogramming you need to do with your subconscious mind.

Your Thoughts Are Real

Thoughts are real; thoughts are powerful. They exist in this world, and they affect it.

Radio waves exist even though you can not see or touch them—you experience the outcome of them by turning on your radio. Brainwaves are the same way. You can measure them with an electro-encephalogram (EEG). They do affect you, and the world around you. You can feel the power of your

thoughts by observing your feelings and body when you are thinking fearful, negative thoughts versus loving, positive thoughts.

You can demonstrate this right now to yourself. Just take a moment to recall the death of a loved one, or a time when you got angry. Your body will feel the same way it did then. Now switch to remembering a beautiful experience with your children, a loved one, an exciting vacation, or even your favorite movie. You'll feel better immediately.

Change Your Thinking

Shift your thought process to becoming more positive, more loving, more forgiving, and more accepting. The sooner you understand the power of positive thoughts and take action to make this shift, the sooner healing can take place. This healing benefits not only you, but also your present or future children and everyone else you encounter in your life.

Negative Thoughts Limit Us

Negative thoughts are blocks. They block creativity. They block the flow of life. They block the energy that flows through your body. They create a sense of feeling tired and rundown.

Thoughts based in fear, anger, frustration, etc. can create tension headaches, stomach problems, aches and pains, and self-destructive addictions. They can even create mental illness, or terminal physical illness, like heart disease and cancer. National best-selling author, Bernie Siegel, MD, has written many books on the effects of thought on the disease process.

"There is now a growing body of evidence that the mind and body, the brain and the immune system are not separate but bound together. We now know, for example, that certain substances produced by the brain transform thoughts and emotions into chemicals, and that these chemicals, in turn, affect the body—either positively or negatively. In short, feelings are chemical and can kill or cure.

—Bernie S. Siegel, MD,
How to Heal Yourself! The Curing Power of Hope, Joy and Inner Peace

Challenges

There are those who say they achieve more by being stressed or by putting pressure on themselves. This can be true. Not all stress is negative. Scientists sometimes make this distinction by calling positive stress "eustress." A challenge, which is a better way of saying a positive stress, can sometimes bring out your best and help you achieve.

You can always achieve more in a positive state. This is an aroused state, but not a negative stress state. You want your children and yourself to achieve, not through stress, or any other emotion based in fear, but through love and a desire to contribute and add value to the world.

Discussion of your state of mind also brings us back to the power of your subconscious mind.

A Cosmic Connection

I believe that in the subconscious arena we have a connection with all other aspects of life.

This "cosmic consciousness," or as Carl Jung described it, "collective unconscious," is the place where all ideas already exist and all life is connected. When we are in a positive, receptive state, we can tie into this cosmic consciousness and bring ideas into our conscious awareness.

This collective consciousness, this connection we have with everything and everyone around us, has been experienced in numerous ways.

> When reading stories of very creative individuals, often times it is stated that the artist or the author becomes empty or inspired and *through them* a work is produced. When later looking at the painting or the written material, the creator is surprised. The collective consciousness flows through the creator, and by experiencing the creation, the creator matures.

One does not have to go too far to find books or stories about experiences that cannot be explained through our five senses.

These include experiences of becoming aware of the death of a family member who lives across the country through a vision or a dream and, the next day, finding out that it really occurred. Intuition is also like this, where there is a "knowing" without factual proof, just a sense of knowing and awareness that something is true.

> *"Consider that our inner world is an energy system. Each urge, desire, emotion, thought, and intuition represents a different wave band of subtle energy. Each of us unconsciously broadcasts the energy of our inner life and receives only that with which we are in tune."*
> —Michael S. Schneider, *A Beginner's Guide to Constructing the Universe*

Developing Our Connections

The point of going into all of this is that we want development to take place on such a level for us and our children. Healthy children have a great openness to life. They are creative and sensitive to life around them. We want our children to remain open to this collective consciousness for new ideas and new creations.

The Confident Subconscious

The quality you want to instill—the one that helps your children to develop healthy subconscious images—is confidence that they can achieve any goal they set their minds to accomplish. They need to feel love and deserving of love, respect, abundance, fulfillment, excitement, and happiness. They need to know that they make a difference.

In creating this powerfully positive, open subconscious mind, your children will be guided to make conscious choices to improve not only themselves but also the world around them. If you can instill these values into your children, then their conscious choices will fulfill this image. They will make conscious choices to live a

WORLD CHANGE

↑

CONSCIOUS CHOICES

↑

**LOVE
RESPECT
HAPPINESS
ABUNDANCE
EXCITEMENT
FULFILLMENT**

very happy and fulfilled life, which I believe is the desire of every parent.

Guiding Children

Creating a positive subconscious image for a child is something we all must do as parents, teachers, coaches, counselors, and anyone else who is interacting with them.

We are all connected. We are all the same. When you help another human being, consider it as helping yourself.

If you can imagine the world four billion years ago, as Carl Sagan wrote in *Cosmos,* everything you see before you came from this world. Solar energy was the only outside addition. It all was generated from the power and energy of the world, the molten lava, the storms, the condensation of water, and the creation of oceans. Tiny organisms were evolving into more complex organisms. All that exists around you came from this primal matter.

When you guide a child in a positive way, you add to the universe in a positive way. There is no greater accomplishment in this world than to positively create and guide a child to become more loving, more open, more confident, more empathic, and more compassionate.

> *"It is sad to see a child who is afraid of the dark...and it is even sadder to see an adult who is afraid of the light."*
> —Bob Proctor

We Are The Universe

Everything in our life is a reflection of us. We must all transform our disempowering subconscious images to live each day with positive thoughts and loving emotions.

The external world is just a mirror of our internal world. If we see many conflicts and problems out there, then we can be sure that we have many conflicts inside. We cannot run from this, though all of us have tried at some point in our lives.

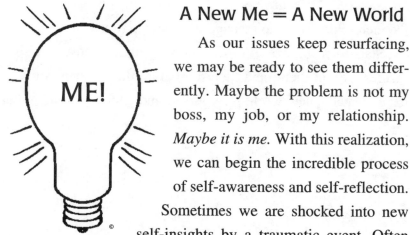

A New Me = A New World

As our issues keep resurfacing, we may be ready to see them differently. Maybe the problem is not my boss, my job, or my relationship. *Maybe it is me.* With this realization, we can begin the incredible process of self-awareness and self-reflection.

Sometimes we are shocked into new self-insights by a traumatic event. Often this leads us to ask what life is all about, is there really a God, and how this can happen to me.

Life has a way of reflecting our internal conflicts and greatest fears into the external world, forcing us to face them to grow as human beings. Many of us flee

"Courage knocked on the door of Fear...Faith opened it...and lo there was no one there."
—Leland Val Van De Wall

initially, then at some point we stop and face our issues.

In Conclusion

When we face our fears, the healing and growth processes start. Our subconscious image is reflected constantly in our daily choices, internal feelings, and the external world. We have the incredible power to reshape our subconscious.

"Computers, with their vast and unique capabilities, demonstrate two main truths: (1) We each have infinite capabilities that we need to learn how to access. (2) There is more to us than we ever suspected or imagined."

—Mark Victor Hansen

Start to recognize your disempowering subconscious self-images, accept them, and then reprogram them. Then you will have created a new world for yourself and all those around you.

6

Emotions

E motions have an incredible influence over human behavior. By taking control of our emotions, we can open up a whole new world for ourselves.

One guiding principle of emotions and behavior has been formulated by philosophers throughout history. This principle is "The Pain and Pleasure Principle." Basically, it states that we avoid pain and seek pleasure. Further, most people will choose to avoid pain over the opportunity to gain pleasure.

The Biology Of Emotions

We avoid pain because we are programmed with an instinct to survive. If we do not survive, then we cannot reproduce and our species will die. Therefore, one of the strongest motivators in us is this desire to avoid pain or "survive."

This programming has been in our genes for over tens of thousands of years. Some would even say that this programming has been present for billions of years (since the beginning of life on this planet).

If we think for a moment of the emotion behind avoiding pain, we are left with only one—fear. The thought that we will somehow suffer creates fear. This is an incredible motivator for action or inaction.

Taking Control Of Your Emotions

The way to start to take control of our lives is by what we link to pain and pleasure.

An example we all can relate to is doing our taxes. The "pain" of pulling all the receipts to-gether, adding the num-bers, filling out the forms, etc. is tremen-dous. For most people, it

> *"You are the sum total of the choices you make."*
> —Wayne Dyer, PhD
> *How to Be a No-Limit Person*

is greater than the relief of having it done. Then as April 15th comes closer, the pain of not having done the taxes and the fear of the penalty increases way above the discomfort of doing the taxes—and the taxes get done.

Proactive Living

The shift that needs to take place is to become proactive instead of reactive. We can create a life based on actions designed to give us pleasure in-stead of constantly reacting to look for the path that will give us the least pain. Living to constantly avoid pain, simply surviving, is not much of a life.

> *We can all learn to live out of a desire to constantly increase our pleasure and happiness in life.*

Every emotion we have is a choice. We can learn to link great pleasure to the actions and goals we desire in life, and pain to the actions we wish to avoid.

Choose Rather Than Project

We have become great projectors of our emotional states. We say things like, "He *makes me* so mad" or "My wife is making me very upset" or "The boss makes me depressed" and so on.

We have given people and external events control over one of the most powerful influences in our lives, our emotions. When we do this, we become like a leaf in the wind, blowing in whatever direction the wind happens to gust.

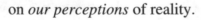

We need to become trees. We must root ourselves with the truth that we are the creators and the masters of our own emotions. We choose the emotions we feel, based on *our perceptions* of reality.

Create Your Reality

When I treat patients who believe that they see the reality of how things are in their relationships or in their lives, I tell them **"There are over 5 billion people in this world and there are over 5 billion realities."**

All human beings perceive life uniquely, through

their past experiences, their genetic programming, and current emotional states. I mention genetic programming because there is no doubt that genetics plays a role in the way we perceive the world.

Creating Reality

Many of the patients we treat in psychiatry have depressive symptoms created by old disempowering beliefs. Once these beliefs shift, the symptoms resolve.

Imagine a two-year-old child who is full of life and energy, finding adventure in the design of a carpet or a leaf. The child accepts what life brings, full of excitement and wonder. The energy of life, spirit of God, cosmic consciousness, or whatever name you wish to give it, flows through this child.

Then it happens. We repeatedly reprimand the child, not out of love but out of anger and frustration.

> *When parents reprimand, it is not so much what is said that matters the most, but the emotion behind what is said. For it is this emotion that children learn to create for themselves.*

So, children are reprimanded and taught that they need to judge the world as to right and wrong, good and bad (and all the messages discussed in the chapter on parenting).

The energy starts to slow down. Children begin to question themselves. Screens or filters have begun to be placed over their eyes. They begin to judge everything instead of flowing and accepting life. They have started developing *their realities.*

Imagine a giant spotlight giving forth an incredibly warm and bright light. As we are reprimanded

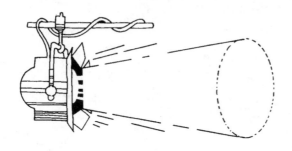

out of anger, over and over again a small screen is put in front of the light. Then we experience rejection and another screen is put up. Then we experience a failure or abandonment and another screen is put up.

Before long, this incredible light is filtered down to just a few small beams. We now perceive reality through this dim, obstructed light—*our* reality.

Programming Children's Realities

Have you ever seen a two-year-old reprimanding his or her stuffed animals? One child in particular comes to mind. The mother, in doing what she had been taught, constantly told her two-year-old daughter what to do. The child was becoming extremely oppositional (more than your typical two-year-old!) to her commands.

The child was exerting her will and reflecting anger in her actions. When playing with her stuffed animals, she put her teddy bears on a shelf, pointed her finger at them and yelled, "Don't move! Don't you move!!"

She did this over and over again. She was already modeling her mother's actions and dealing with her own anxiety by playing it out. Any time children have built up emotions like anxiety or frustration, we can see it unfold in their play on a daily basis.

> *All perception begins in the mind of the individual. The world is just a reflection of that perception.*

If a person was abused as a child, the perception may be that, "I am a victim." Then, as people live their adolescent and adult lives, they perceive many events as someone or something "always picking on me" or "happening to me." They ask questions like, "Why does this always happen to me?" or "What did I do to deserve this?"

All of the questions focus on the problem, keeping the person receiving more of the same since they are focused on the problem instead of the solution.

Love And Happiness

The incredible news is that we can—and will—remove the negative screens that dim our lives.

> "In the beginning was the Word; the Word was in God's presence, and the Word was God.
>
> "Through Him all things came into being, apart from Him nothing came to be. The Word became flesh and made His dwelling among us...filled with enduring love....Of His fullness we have all had a share—love following upon love."
>
> —John, *The New Testament*

"Brahma is the original creature born out of the energy of the Supreme Lord, and from Brahma all ...are manifest."

—Bhagavad-gita, *As It Is*

Could love be our true essence? Could love be the form of highest vibration through which all of creation is manifested?

We know through physics that everything in the physical world vibrates. We also know that directed energy is the final building block of the universe.

In The Beginning

Mysticism, Eastern thought, and other philosophies say that in the beginning there was the void, only one God, nothing separate. Then the first vibration appeared, love. Then the rest unfolded through God which formed the universe. If this is the truth, then our true essence, or highest vibration, may, in fact, be love.

If our true essence is love, then we would all expect to operate better in a state of love. This is true for most of us. There are those whose lives were so traumatized that love and affection may cause tremendous conflict. But once the conflict is worked through, love can have this impact.

Our goal in life is to be happy. Think of why you work, make money, have a family, friends, a home, car, clothes, and other material things, play sports, or entertain yourself. All these things in the end are designed to give us happiness.

Whether Mother Teresa or Donald Trump, we are driven to those things that fulfill us, that make us happy. Mother Teresa is fulfilled and happy by self-sacrifice and devoting her life to helping some of the least fortunate in the world. Donald Trump is fulfilled and happy by being the best, owning the biggest, and being a master in the art of making the big deal.

I believe the ultimate expression of this happiness is a state of love. We are programmed to strive toward our essence.

Daily Miracles

The book, *A Course in Miracles,* and a simplified understanding of parts of the course by Gerald Jampolsky, MD, in his book, *Love Is Letting Go of Fear*, breaks down all emotion into love and the opposite, fear.

Imagine we are conceived in a pure potential form ready to be directed by our environment and express our full human and genetic potential. The consciousness or energy of life flowing through us is like a river channelling the water through us. One canal is love; the other, is fear. The energy flows in the canal and is converted into the emotion and becomes expressed in the positive and negative ways listed.

ENERGY OF LIFE

LOVE

JOYFUL
CARING
CURIOUS
HELPFUL
SHARING

FEAR

HATEFUL
REJECTED
ANXIOUS
JUDGMENTAL
ANGRY

The energy converted into love becomes expressed as confidence, happiness, caring, sharing, curiosity, learning, empathy, compassion, etc. The energy converted into fear becomes expressed in the form of anger, frustration, disappointment, rejection, loneliness, depression, anxiety, etc.

We fluctuate between both canals on a daily basis. But most of us are predominantly in one or the other canal or state. We then perceive our world through this state, finding many reasons to **justify** our feelings.

Negative ➤ Negative

If we are in an angry state, then we will focus on all the behaviors of our spouse that we *believe* upset us and react, justified by what we perceive. In the angry state, we see all the piles around the house and feel how neglected or taken advantage of we are. We see the dishes in the sink and feel no one cares about us, or "I am doing all the work in this family."

Love ➤ Love

If we are in an emotional state based on love, then we will perceive the behaviors that support that emotion. Our emotional state becomes a screen or filter through which our perceptions flow.

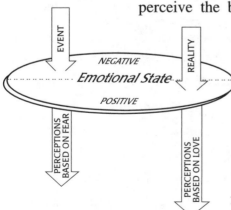

What we see is filtered so we perceive those things that support what we already feel. If we shift, we shift the filters of perception and perceive a different world.

Our emotional states are based on our focus at the moment. If we think of a baby's soft skin, a baby's smile, a child's laughter, the embrace of a lover, or our first kiss, we can instantly create the emotions based on love.

If we shift to thoughts of terrorists blowing up a building and killing innocent people, or someone poisoning the candy they gave out on Halloween, we can instantly feel emotions based on fear.

Did you notice the difference in your breath, body posture, facial expression, and muscle tension as you read this? Remember, there are 5 billion people in this world and most of them live in peace, harmony, and love. (You'll understand this statement better once you read the Reprogramming chapter.)

Thoughts Create Energy

Every thought has a corresponding physical and emotional manifestation. Our thoughts affect our perception of the world.

> *The energy or cosmic consciousness flows in, we convert the energy into a thought, the thoughts then affect our bodies and emotions, and we perceive the world through this preframed moment.*

Look at the picture on the opposite page. *Now turn the page* and take a look at the next picture and describe what you see.

You would probably describe the woman as about 25 to 35 years old, attractive, fashionable, and maybe even sophisticated. A single young man might wish to ask her out.

Now what would you say if I told you that this person is between 60 to 80 years old or older? She has a huge nose, looks rather sad, and a young man would definitely not be romantically interested. You would respond, "You have to be out of your mind. She is beautiful, and in her thirties at the very most." We could go on like this, each supporting and arguing the "facts."

Now look at the third picture on page 87. Now go back to the second picture on page 85. Do you see the picture I was describing. This is a clear example of how we preframe the world we perceive through our preframed minds. Then we call it "reality."

This is why I have used the statement, "There are over 5 billion people in this world and there are over 5 billion realities."

The secret to love and happiness is to preframe each moment with love and happiness. Don't *look* for it. Let it *flow from* you.

Thoughts And Emotions

We can begin preframing ourselves by reprogramming our subconscious minds and by focusing our conscious minds. We can shift our emotions of the moment by shifting our thoughts.

Notice that there is an interaction, a flow back and forth between thoughts and

emotions. Thoughts form, and are
formed, by emotions and physiology.

An example of this is Jennifer, a
young adult female, who reported this experience with a
close female friend, Sara. Sara
was in tremendous pain from
recent dental work.

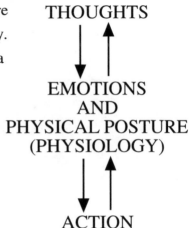

THOUGHTS

EMOTIONS
AND
PHYSICAL POSTURE
(PHYSIOLOGY)

ACTION

Thought: Sara is in great
↓   pain and needs help.
Emotion: love, compassion, empathy.
↓
Action: went over to care for Sara.

Now notice Jennifer's changing feelings, after
caring for her close friend, because of her
preframing, or her prior programs.

Thought: I am becoming too close, this is
↓   too intimate.
Emotion: scared, uncomfortable.
↓
Action: create distance by not calling or
            visiting for a while.

Why The Change?

When delving into the deeper conflicts behind
Jennifer's conscious thoughts, we discovered subconscious fears of being abandoned or rejected.

If we operate from these fears, we will often
reject or leave a relationship before the other person
rejects us. Or, we will set it up so the other person

leaves. When this happens, we have verified our fears, "I knew this was going to happen." Over time, our friend may become frustrated with the on-again-off-again type of relationship and leave the friendship. Jennifer would then have created the very thing she feared.

After Jennifer recognized her subconscious fears, she was then guided to connect them with past traumas, or, as you may have noticed, I would rather call them challenges.

This patient recalled a boyfriend she dated for two years in high school. Then he began dating someone else. Even deeper, she remembered being rejected in first grade by a group of classmates who did not want her to work on "their dinosaur project."

And deeper still (at the base of the iceberg), her mother gave her up for adoption. She never knew her mother and fantasizes that her mother, like in "'Miss Saigon' gave me up for a better life before she killed herself." And at an even deeper level, Jennifer's mother possibly conveyed negative thoughts and feelings to Jennifer while Jennifer was in her womb.

A Better Perception

We then worked through how the present event could have unfolded another way.

        Thought: Sara is in great pain and needs help.
        ↓
        Emotion: love, compassion, empathy.
        ↓
        Action: went over to care for Sara.

then...

        Thought: She really needed my help and appreciated my thoughtfulness. We are great friends.
        ↓
        Emotion: love, happiness, gratitude.
        ↓
        Action: spend more time building a closer and more meaningful friendship.

Remember, the closer we are to ourselves (i.e., the more we understand and love ourselves), the closer we can become to others.

The next question that comes to mind is how to remove the fears that have lead up to the disempowering, distance-creating, thoughts.

Let's go back to the idea that all feelings are based on love or fear. There are many steps we can take to live in the state of love. The first step in producing this shift is not to judge anything that occurs.

Practice Nonjudgment

The scribes and the Pharisees led a woman forward who had been caught in adultery. "Teacher," they said to him, "this woman has been caught in the act of adultery. In the law, Moses ordered such women to be stoned. What do you have to say about

the case?" Jesus bent down and started tracing on the ground with his finger. "Let the man among you who has no sin be the first to cast a stone at her."

Practice Nonjudgment

A wise teacher of Eastern thought and meditation was sitting around a camp fire with his students. He was teaching his great wisdom, as a grasshopper appeared next to the fire.

The master reached over and pulled out one of the flaming sticks from the fire and touched the back of the grasshopper, a sizzle was heard and the grasshopper leaped from the burn and jumped into the distance.

The students became enraged at their teacher. "How could you do this? You have preached year after year on nonviolence, peace, and bringing no harm to anything in life. Yet you burned the back of that grasshopper. This is an outrage."

The master replied, "If I had not done so, the next leap of the grasshopper would have been into the fire, and it would have died."

Flow

The point of these stories is that we often become stuck in the process of judging everything around us. This can remove the free flow of life. We judge, and thereby separate ourselves from events.

We have all done the wrong thing at some point, or judged too quickly before all the evidence was in. Many of us live our lives in moment-to-moment judgements. This process of judgment keeps us separate from the flow of life. We put up barriers or walls between us and others. Once the barrier or wall is up, we feel safe but alone. We can all begin to let the walls down.

In Conclusion

We need to take total responsibility for our emotions, and therefore gain total control. By perceiving the world through love rather than fear, we will be happier. We will create fewer barriers and become more flowing with the energy of life.

7

Emotional Mastery

Life often presents us with the "back of the tapestry." We see knots, loose strings, colors that do not match, and images that do not make much sense, and we feel uncomfortable.

If we stay open, stand back, remain non-judgmental, and look for the lesson to be learned, we will eventually make it to the other side. Now standing in front of the tapestry we will behold the beauty and magnificence of life.

The only way to become angry in this world is to judge. Judgment, formulated in the preframed conscious mind, prevents us from learning, growing, and expanding as we did as children.

Child-like Adaptability

Think of the endless energy of a two-and-one-half-year-old, the curiosity, and the massive learning that takes place.

We could take any baby or young child and place them in any part of the world. With time, they would be speaking and writing the language of that country. Just thinking of this may

create fear in many adults—a judgment process of, "I could not do
that."

Children do not naturally judge. The
fears, judgments, and ideas of those
around them are transferred to them.

We teach them to fear spiders and
snakes, or dislike different types of people
or events. Once the program is set, they
now can have the thoughts that they were
preprogrammed to think. This creates the
emotions that come from these thoughts. Then they
act accordingly.

Relatives

Parents   Society

Beliefs,
Judgments,
and Fears

↓

CHILD

Obsessive Beliefs

Steve, a 34-year-old married man, came to me
with severe obsessive and compulsive symptoms.
Medication had failed in the past. His obsessive
thoughts were that he had to clean and organize
everything in his office, bedroom, and garage "to be
perfect" before he could focus on his work.

Impossible To Work

After spending several hours compulsively
cleaning and organizing, he would sit down to work
and, within five to fifteen minutes, the obsessive
thoughts would again arise. He would have to stop
work and do the entire routine again to have any
peace.

He would have to spend twelve to fourteen

hours on his job in order to get two hours of work done. He worked both in his home and out of town. He also would be obsessive and compulsive in his hotel room, and with his suitcases. His life was difficult, especially with his wife, Sally, and their two-and-one-half-year-old daughter, Faith.

Can you imagine what his wife could do if she were upset with him? "Honey, the garage seems a little disorganized," just after he spent an hour cleaning and organizing it! Or she could tell their daughter, "Why don't you play in daddy's office today."

What a life! People actually live with these types of symptoms for years before seeking help.

Faulty Thinking

We looked back into his life to find causes besides the well known genetic or biologic cause of obsessive compulsive disorder. To understand these deeper conflicts, we processed through his emotions.

Steve was out of town one day and received a call from his wife. Sally, who was also going through her own growth process, was very upset and angry. She told Steve, who paraphrased for me, "My life is being wasted away, I cannot do anything except take care of our child. I have no life or independence while *you* travel for your job, are productive, and have fun." His response was initially supportive. When the angry and frustrated comments continued from his wife, he:

> Thought:　I should be there. This job is interfering
> ↓　　　　with my life and my relationship.
> Emotion:　Anger and guilt.
> ↓
> Action:　　Look for another job.

Learned Guilt

After listening and being supportive, I responded: "When did you first feel guilty?"

Steve replied, "All my life. My mother made me feel guilty to motivate me." He went on to describe the obsessive and compulsive cleaning and organizing they had to do before having any fun. His mother was as obsessive and compulsive as he was and she recruited the kids to help.

The guilt came in when he was told he did not care about the family if he did not clean, or that he was selfish or lazy. As a child, the anger was building and suppressed (pushed down) because he could not do the things many children were permitted to do. He was obsessively cleaning and organizing instead of playing, socializing, and laughing.

Taking Charge

There are many lessons in this story. First is the lesson of **taking responsibility for your emotions and not your partner's**. I will discuss this in great detail in the Relationship chapter.

Steve felt responsible for his wife's anger and frustration until he realized he only needed to take responsibility for his own anger and guilt. His wife needed to deal with her own emotions. He understood and was able to make this shift.

He also has begun to reduce the guilt by raising the level of when he would feel guilty. We all have rules on when we experience certain emotions. Some of his rules to feel guilt were:

- when I upset my wife
- when I upset my mother
- when I don't do what others expect of me

With these rules, many of us would feel guilty every day. Steve does not control the emotions of his wife, mother, or "others." He is setting himself up to feel guilty by depending on their reactions. Living with these rules, he is not in control of his emotional life. Since guilt is not a desired feeling, we need to raise the level at which we will experience it by changing our rules.

Here's one simple key to happiness. Create a belief system, a set of rules, that makes it easy to experience positive emotions and much more difficult to experience negative emotions! For most people, the opposite is true!

New Rules

Steve used to feel guilty throughout the day. His new rule for guilt is, "I will only feel guilty if God comes down to earth and tells me to my face that I am a worthless human being. Short of that life just happens."

Since this event is not likely to occur, Steve will not feel guilt in his life once he fully integrates this new belief. And that is all that it is, a belief—just like his disempowering rules, they were only beliefs!

Control Your Own Rules

Only believe those things that will give you power and control over your emotions and thoughts.

We also worked on the rules he had in his mind for perfection and how to change his belief structure about this idea. He described the exact way all his papers, books, machines, files, chairs, etc. had to be in order to be perfect. If one thing was tilted, or in the "wrong place," it was no longer perfect.

His new rules: "If the desk was still in the office, that is perfect!! If the carpet is still on the bedroom floor, that is perfect!! If the garage door is still on the garage, now that is perfect!!"

Control The Past

Our current work is focused on Steve associating the remaining guilt or obsessive thoughts to his mother's behavior in the past. When his negative thoughts arise he now tells himself ,"No, Mom, everything is just fine" or "Everything is just perfect."

Since he has been wanting both consciously and subconsciously to ignore her (I am being very kind here), this association will be easy for him to install and practice.

> *"The law of self-fulfilling prophecy says that you get what you expect. So why not create great expectations and the highest vision possible of yourself and the world?"*
> —Mark Victor Hansen

With a combination of therapy and medication, Steve has been, at times, feeling happier and more liberated than ever before in his adult life. The goal, which I believe is attainable for Steve, is to eventually be off medication and doing great.

The Family System

Sally, Steve's wife, also has been going through some rule changes. In order for her to feel happy and fulfilled, she thought she had to be working in "some profession," making money, socializing with adults at "some job," getting dressed in professional clothes in the morning, etc., etc.

She also wants to lose weight and sees taking care of Faith as stopping her from all of these things.

Actually, Sally had a great desire to stay home and take care of her beautiful daughter. She was being emotionally drained by these opposing beliefs and desires. She realized that her true desire was to feel happy and fulfilled. We just needed to associate all the feelings of happiness and fulfillment to taking care of

Faith—which, by the way, many of us know is the most important job any person could have in this world!

From Conflict To Joy

Sally loved her daughter but had "programs" running in her head about what her life should be. Her new rules for happiness and fulfillment are:

- when I teach my daughter, or
- when I play with my daughter, or
- when I clean the house, or
- when I am supportive of my husband

Take Control

Notice that Sally is in control of the action behind each rule. Therefore, she is in control of her experience and the emotion that results from doing the actions!

We can, and need to, make a list a mile long of the rules by which we feel happiness and fulfillment. But these need to be rules where we control the action.

Besides the shifts above, Sally also desired to lose weight. She was able to associate keeping up and playing with her two-and-a-half-year-old as exercise rather than a burden. She was now able to add this to her weight-loss program.

Sally's Old Beliefs

We judge the world through programmed or preframed mind sets. Aaron Beck, originator of cognitive therapy, saw emotions and behavior largely determined by the way we structure our world. We need to change our mind sets to empower ourselves. We

> *"Habits of thinking need not be forever. One of the most significant findings in psychology in the last twenty years is that individuals can choose the way they think."*
>
> —Aaron Beck, *Love Is Never Enough*

must change our rules for what it takes for us to experience certain emotions.

Following are some of the rules in Sally's mind.

In order for me to feel fulfilled:

- I must have a job.
- I must make money.
- I must be a professional.

But I also have a two-and-a-half-year-old and want to raise her. This belief system would cause emotional conflicts in any of us.

This is just a simple example of someone who is actually emotionally healthy and strong. Sally, like many of us, has these disempowering beliefs that create chaos in her emotional state and affect her behavior.

What Are Your Rules?

Everyone needs to look at their rules for happiness, love, fulfillment, and the other emotions they desire. The rules for experiencing love are a great example of how many of us give our control and power to other people. In doing this, we rarely experience the emotion of love. Here are some of the rules that female patients have shared about love.

In order for me to experience love:

- My husband needs to tell me he loves me at least three times a day.
- We must make love every night.
- He has to be there for me all the time.
- He has to give me flowers once a week.

- My children have to listen to everything I say.
- My children have to tell me they love me twice a day.

The next question that needs to be asked, once we write out our rules, is who is in control of those rules? The obvious answer is my husband and children! These rules turn over the power of experiencing love to others.

Rewriting Your Own Scripts

The key to living in a state of love and happiness is to be in control of the rules that determine when you experience those states. More empowering rules to adopt are:

I will experience love when I:

- tell my husband I love him or
- make love with my husband or
- give a gift to my husband or children or
- take care of my family's needs or
- tell my children I love them or
- listen to my children or
- exercise or
- nourish my body with healthy food or
- see the sunshine or
- see the rain or
- receive a massage, etc., etc.

Take Control Of Your Rules

We can experience love and happiness all day long if we create the rules to do so.

Who is in charge of these new rules? You are! You can now live with a new set of beliefs that give you the power and control over your life.

Better Rules
1. I will determine the threshhold for experiencing emotions.
2. I will feel rejected only when a million people tell me, to my face, in a single day, that I'm worthless...otherwise life just happens.

We must redo our rules because we did not create them. We were trained and learned these rules from those around us.

If our parents are or were not living an incredible, loving, happy and fulfilled life, then we definitely need to redo the rules that were passed down to us.

Negative Emotions

Anger, frustration, disappointment, and other emotions we wish to avoid must also be looked at.

Negative emotions can be great tools for us to learn about ourselves. But we also need rules for when we experience them. We can reduce our negative emotions by raising the threshold to such a level that we rarely have to feel this way.

In Steve's example, he raised his guilt threshold to be, "I will feel guilty only if God comes down and tells me to my face that I am a worthless human being."

One married women raised her rejection level to, "A million people telling me to my face, in a single day, that I am a terrible human being and do not deserve to be alive." Only then would she feel rejected. "Short of this, life just happens."

Write Down Your Rules

Now it is your turn to write out your current rules for the emotions you desire *and* those you wish to avoid. Then rewrite your rules for the emotions you wish to create so they are easier to experience. And raise the threshold for those you wish to avoid. We all must do this.

Shift From Judgment To Love

The only way to feel angry is to judge the events in our lives. This happens when we move from being in the moment to judging the moment.

We can live a life of abundant energy and love by just letting go of this judgment process. It consumes a tremendous amount of thought and emotional energy. Stop judging that this is good or bad, fair or unfair, stupid, etc. Just be in the moment and flow. Direct the things you have influence over, then let go.

Mary's Story Of Anger

Many people use anger as a motivator to achieve, or to become strong or aggressive to produce a result they desire.

Mary was one such patient. She is an adult single women who, since birth, has had cerebral palsy. She was so determined, proud, and disciplined that she worked her entire life even though she had very little mobility in her right arm.

Overcoming Adversity

Mary mastered her work with her left arm. But over time she developed problems in this arm, and lost a majority of its functioning. She then entered a phase of depression.

All her life she struggled against this "disability," never wanting to be labeled as dis-

Sigmund Freud called depression anger directed at oneself, and suicide the ultimate expression of that anger.

abled or ever applying for benefits, not even a disability parking sticker. She took great pride in her work and her productivity.

When the work was removed because of the loss in functioning of her good arm, the anger and frustration were directed at herself and depression unfolded.

Anger ➤ Motivation

Mary used anger and frustration as motivators to achieve. Here is an example of how easily she thought her way into an angry state. She drove past a nursing home and began to think:

Thought:

↓

How cruel the nursing home was that took care of my mother. I was not there for her; I was not a good daughter. How awful nursing

	homes are to abuse and beat their residents, etc.
Emotion:	Anger, guilt.
↓	
Action:	Prayed.

Shifting To Love

After listening to her, I asked her, "What does getting angry do for you?"

She replied, "It makes me stronger and aggressive and I achieve more. I do what I need to do." She then went through her history of how her anger and frustration were used to help her get through school and her work.

We then worked on creating a belief that happiness, love, curiosity, and a desire to learn and grow could also guide us to achieve. These attributes can be positive and assertive.

Love Vs. Anger

Many of us have linked pain and weakness to the emotion of love. This is the most disempowering association we can have in our lives.

Love is the most powerful force in this world. Weakness is based in fear, insecurity, lack of confidence, and not feeling you

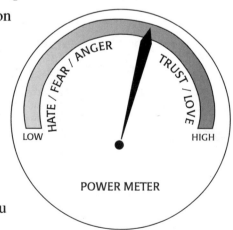

deserve to be heard. Weakness is based on a belief that you are not abundant and powerful. This is weakness, not love.

In order for us to use anger as an emotion to motivate, we must focus on the negative in situations. That is exactly what Mary was doing as you can see from the example. She was a master at putting herself in an angry state, and adding some guilt.

A Positive Approach

Mary is a Jehovah's Witness. She gave me a book on her faith and wanted me to read the book. We made a deal. If she was able to go one week with only positive thoughts, then I would read the book!

She had the best several weeks in a long time with more happiness than she could recall. Friends even noticed how she looked brighter, happier, and seemed less burdened. After a month, she still had not gone a full week, but was doing much better at shifting her focus and using love and happiness as motivators rather than using anger and guilt.

The other obvious challenge Mary is working through is the physical limitation she has lived with her entire life: letting go of the anger toward the doctor whom she feels could have delivered her sooner and with less trauma.

Letting go, accepting, and forgiving are valuable practices we must apply to our lives.

Learn To Forgive

We must forgive those whom we believe have hurt us or misled us. We have all hurt others. Sometimes realizing this helps us forgive others for hurting us.

We can take another example from the life of Jesus Christ, who was dying on the cross when a Roman soldier threw a spear in His side. His response as written in the Bible was, "Father forgive them for they know not what they do."

The moment the event happened, He was able to forgive and stay in a state of love. Anger and other emotions based in fear did not even manifest.

Shape Yourself

We must see life as a gift. The events in life all have two faces: empowering and disempowering. We must train ourselves to become great leaders who are able to find the best in every situation and person.

Ask great questions

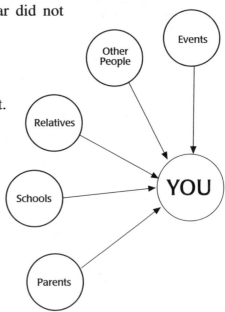

like, "How can I learn and grow from this experience and how can I use this experience to improve my life?"

We are all like a mass of clay with incredible potential to become an unlimited number of things. We are then molded by life, our parents (or lack of parents), schools, relatives, other people in our lives, and the events in our lives.

We, as adults, now have the ability to forgive not only others but ourselves. Dr. Rahul Mehra, a close friend and fellow Child and Adolescent Psychiatrist, had a grandfather who was an attorney and a philosopher. When Rahul graduated from the Child Fellowship at The University of South Florida Medical Center, he passed out a scroll from his grandfather. The opening verse was, "Forgive everyone for everything and forgive yourself for everything and you will remove illness from your body."

"Forgive everyone for everything and forgive yourself for everything and you will remove illness from your body."

In Conclusion

Our emotions are powerful influences on our lives. But they depend on how we frame, or interpret, the situations we are in.

You can shift from fear to love through:

- changing your rules, and your belief system
- eliminating judgment, or if you must judge, then judging positively
- practicing forgiveness, letting go, and acceptance

The sooner you start, the happier you'll be!

8

Growing Through Relationships

Relationships are the most powerful experiences we have to help us develop. The closer we become to another person, the more we grow.

The world is a mirror of our internal state. A relationship brings that mirror very close. It helps us stare face-to-face into our issues.

Initially, in the face of this intensity, most of us run because the pain, anger, frustration, and fear are too great to face. So we go from relationship to relationship **linking** the anger, frustration, and other negative emotions to the person we are with. We decide that this person is not right for us.

Relationship Mirrors

By entering into relationships, we are beginning the process of looking at ourselves. What we do with the emotions that arise depends on how insightful we are. **We must acknowledge that every feeling is ours and take full responsibility.** This will empower us to look inside ourselves to find the true cause of the feeling and begin the process of letting go.

We blame others until we become frustrated by the process and ask a different question: "Maybe it is not the other person—maybe I need to look at myself?" When we reach this stage, we begin the process of self-enlightenment.

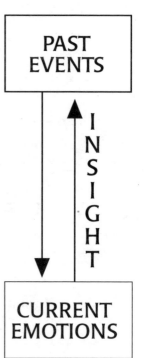

The Therapeutic Relationship

One intense and, at times, uncomfortable type of relationship is therapy. Because it's what I was trained to do, it's an easy example for me to use.

In traditional analytic psychotherapy, as people develop relationships with therapists, their issues start to surface. The stronger the feelings in the therapeutic relationship, the more people come face to face with their issues. Anger, frustration, disappointment, etc. are often projected onto the therapist. (This is called transference.)

The therapist interprets the material to help the patient gain conscious awareness of conflicts. A process of connecting the past events to the current feelings takes place and insight is gained.

Past Challenges

Most overwhelming negative emotions have at their roots a painful childhood event, or perceived failure.

This challenging event may be as obvious as abuse or as subtle as the birth of a sibling.

The Sibling Example

Thinking as an adult, it may be hard to understand how the birth of a sibling could create strong fears of rejection or abandonment. Imagine what a three-and-a-half-year-old boy feels when his mother who was there supporting, engaging, and playing with him becomes preoccupied with a difficult pregnancy. And after the birth, she is preoccupied and focused on the newborn.

The process can be very traumatic to this child. It can create fears of rejection, abandonment, and insecurity that last for life, or until they have been resolved.

Emotional Memory

Prior to the age of four to five we cannot recall great details of the events in our lives. Our limited vocabulary and conscious memory (that is, prior to this early stimulation program) make it difficult to code details of the events of our lives.

What we do recall are emotions. Old emotions can, and do, interfere with current relationships. These feeling memories are experienced in our lives on a daily basis in numerous encounters.

Live In The Present

Think about the emotions you experience on a daily basis.

If you realize that a majority of your emotions are based in fear or anger, then you are living through past painful events and perceived failures. You are experiencing the present as if it were the past.

We all have as our basic nature love and happiness.

We start with positive emotions. Then challenges occur. A sibling is born, other events take place, or we "fail." Our natural love and happiness are buried by emotions such as anger, frustration, disappointment, and fear.

Living In The Past

Many of us are living our present lives through the past, holding on to *what we know*.

They spend their time mostly looking forward to the past.
—John Osborn in *Look Back in Anger*

What do we really know? We know our past, what we were taught, and what we have experienced in life. Yet life occurs in the present.

The present and the future are unknown. Most of us are uncomfortable with the unknown, therefore we don't live in the present. We drag our past into the present because we know it.

We react in the present moment from our past knowledge and past emotions. We are thinking and acting based on our past. Therefore the results we receive are the same as we received in the past.

To paraphrase Albert Einstein, "The definition of insanity is doing the same thing over and over again and expecting a new result."

How To Happily Achieve

Many of us strive for happiness by achieving a goal that we believe will make us happy. Yet once the goal is achieved, any happiness is fleeting. We then turn to the next goal, and so on.

The answer is that there is no path *to* happiness. Happiness *is* the path. It is right inside yourself.

There is no place to go. What we need to do is to remove the anger, frustration, fear, and other negative thoughts. Then we can let the beauty of the moment, the excitement of the unknown, the massive joy and love inside envelop us.

Have Faith In The Present

The present is all that matters. Who knows what will happen to us five minutes from now?

As this is being written in May, 1996, a plane crashed, killing all the passengers and crew. How many people on that plane were worried about the future, about work, or some family or financial problem? How many people on that plane were feeling anxious, guilty, or frustrated about their lives or their past?

The only moment that matters is this moment. Nothing else exists. If you fill this moment with negativity because you are dwelling on the past or future, that is your choice.

"Live each day as if you will die tomorrow, learn each day as if you will live forever."
—Mahatma Gandhi

Take Control

> *Neither God nor anyone else will stop us because we are in control of our thoughts. That is our one true freedom and the only control that truly matters!*

Remove the fear and have faith that life will unfold as it should. We must learn to trust and enjoy the process of life.

Be Happy

Everyone can achieve more in a state of happiness. We work and think more efficiently and creatively. Happiness also brings love. In a state of love we have better relations with those around us.

Have Faith

No one reading this knows for certain if he or she will be alive five minutes from now, or one minute from now.

We can all speculate but not know with 100% certainty. When you last drove your car did you know with 100% certainty that the brakes would work the next time you pressed them?

No, you had faith that they would work based on past experience. You had so much faith they would work that you probably never even thought about it.

> *Let us expand this realm of faith and trust to all areas of our lives over which we have little influence. Yes, we can make sure we have brake fluid at the proper times and check the brakes if there are signs of wear and tear. Then let go.*

We can plan, invest, and stride toward goals. Then we need to happily achieve them living in the moment, not frustrated because we have not achieved the goal yet.

The universe works on its own time schedule, not ours.

Every event and person in our lives can help us look at ourselves to become more tolerant, loving, and enlightened human beings. Live with the idea that the person with you at each moment is the most important person in the world.

Forgive And Move Forward

We must all forgive our parents, others whom we feel caused us pain, and ourselves.

"Let us forget and forgive injuries."
—Miguel de Cervantes;
Don Quixote

We must ask better questions. If we were abused growing up, we will only continue to feel pain and weakness if we ask questions like, "Why am I a victim?" or "Why did this have to happen to me?"

Better questions are:

- "How can I learn from this?"
- "How can I grow from this?"
- "How can I use this experience in my life?"

These questions will give us power and take our lives to the next level. We must focus on solutions, not problems.

Look Inside

When anger, frustration, rejection, and disappointment arise, don't blame something outside yourself. Look within.

When you have negative feelings, try to understand if they are remnants of past experiences.

- What is it about me or my past that is still guiding me to feel this way?
- My father left me when I was young. Is this a remnant of feeling abandoned or rejected?
- My mother was an alcoholic and no matter what I did, I was put down. Is this the reason I feel I am not good enough?

We must all work through our issues. If we are not happy most of the day, we have issues to work on.

If we think and act the same as we did yesterday, we will get the same results.

Remember the Einstein quote. If we desire our lives to enter a new level of happiness, love, passion, wealth, and connectedness, then we must think and act differently.

Prepare For Progress

Make the necessary changes in your life. Focus on the goals you desire by using the questions that will be discussed in the chapter on Reprogramming. Prepare your mind to see the opportunities that cross your path on a daily basis.

The thoughts, attitudes, and beliefs you carry with you will attract both your greatest fears and your desires.

A tuning fork that is tapped will cause an untouched tuning fork of the same frequency to vibrate.

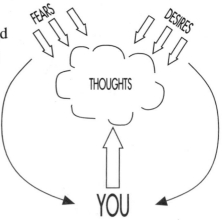

The vibration is carried and the same-frequency tuning fork begins to vibrate. **We are the same; we attract to us those individuals and events that resonate to what we project in our thoughts.**

Though it is true, not everything that happens to us was attracted by us. Life should be seen as an awesome learning and loving experience, not an experience of fear.

Everything happens for a reason. As Albert Einstein stated, "The most incomprehensible thing about the universe is that it is comprehensible."

A Personal Example

I have been through many relationships and, as most of us do, I projected all "my stuff" onto the person I was with.

Finally, I was "ready" in my life. My wife Susan, who was a medical student at the time, was also prepared for a relationship. We began dating and the issues started flying.

I have had a fear of being abandoned. You see, the three-and-a-half year old boy described previously was me. My mother was very sick carrying my younger brother and therefore was less available to me. I unknowingly carried this fear and insecurity buried in my unconscious when entering relationships.

When my feelings grew stronger in a new relationship, as we became closer, anger arose. Then I would look *outside myself* and find several "reasons" to be angry and know this relationship would never work. (It took me over 16 years as an adult to realize this.)

Maybe It Is Me

When we feel angry, we **focus** on the "negative" aspects of the person we are with.

We can all find faults in others. So after I accumulated enough data about the "faults" in a new relationship, I pulled out.

Susan was the first person who was able to help me see that my anger was coming from me and not all the "stuff" I projected onto her. (Also, I was prepared to listen.) This took some time and willingness on my part to look at myself, and patience on Susan's part.

I began to see things differently. *Maybe she is right. What if it is me?*

Bingo! As soon as this shift took place, my emotional state began to improve. I began to take responsibility for my emotions. It is a good thing that our first year of dating was a long-distance relationship that gave us breaks from the intensity. (She spent her first year of psychiatry residency at Duke University Medical Center while I was at the University of South Florida Medical Center.)

They're Our Emotions

We have both come to realize that we are totally responsible for our emotions. We need to look within for the deeper truth and not blame the superficial external "causes" we have deluded ourselves into believing.

We all have these smoldering "campfires" inside. The external event (for example, the car that pulls out in front of us in

traffic) is just like a breeze to the smouldering fire. The fire is ignited, we feel it, and quickly associate the anger with the "@%!#" who just pulled out in front of us. We ventilate, think we are justified, and may still be on fire for a while. Then the anger goes back to just smoldering again, waiting to be ignited at the next "cause."

The truth is that all of us have experienced painful events growing up. Any current sign of abuse, neglect, or being taken advantage of ignites our fires. We may have been ignored growing up, and a current incident represents being ignored again.

Being ignored growing up is the truth and the source of the anger—*not* all of the superficial associations we have assumed to be the truth, or the cause of the anger.

You Can't Always Tell What The Issue Is

It was a week before Susan and I were to marry. We were living in Tampa, Florida. I worked in a hospital one hour away in Largo. One morning I awoke at 5 am and was at work by 7 am. On this particular day I was very busy and did not return home until after 7:30 pm.

Susan also had a long day and was still not home. She enjoys cooking and does most of it, but I

decided to make a Mediterra-
nean dish of lentils and rice
that takes approximately 45
to 50 minutes to prepare. My
wife came home while I was
cooking and she was pleas-
antly surprised and grateful.

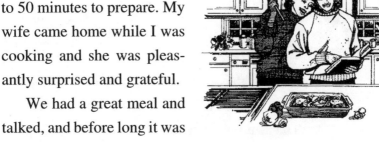

We had a great meal and
talked, and before long it was
11:30. I was beat and prepared to retire. While I was
brushing my teeth, Susan appeared distraught for
reasons that are still unclear to both of us and
attempted to engage me in conversation.

The "Wrong" Response

I was very tired and tried to listen but I could not
understand her point. I told her I was tired and
wanted to go to bed. She persisted. I was at the point
of being delirious and I laughed slightly about the
situation. To her, this indicated I was insensitive,
uncaring, and unsupportive.

Her Reaction

She was so upset by my brief laughter, she
grabbed the glass I was using for rinsing and threw
the water on me.

This struck me as ridiculous and I laughed even
more about the situation which, as you can imagine,
did not help matters.

"Don't give me that logic stuff. If I wanted logic I would have married Plato."

Her Overreaction

As I was drying myself and bent down to wipe the tile, I looked up to see Susan holding a bucket full of water which she then dumped on me.

I was soaked and laughed again, though not as much. I understood that I was in control of my emotions and she was going through some issue of her own. I changed my clothes, put towels down on the tile, and still felt great about my day.

I knew she was struggling with some inner turmoil. I kissed her and wished her a good night and went to bed.

Listening Is Often The Key

Susan stayed up for two more hours processing what was going on within herself. In the morning she apologized for her behavior and we discussed the true issues of feeling unheard and unsupported.

The issue of not being listened to by a male figure was one of her childhood issues. Her father was a physician who was very busy with his practice and very demanding of his children. He rarely expressed his acceptance of her, and she felt he was always too busy to listen. She realized that had been the true issue and not the superficial event that triggered the internal smoldering camp fire to ignite.

Own Your Emotions

We all have these smoldering camp fires. We must take full responsibility for our emotions and not accept responsibility for the emotions of others.

If I had responded to Susan in anger, we would have argued into the night, with neither one of us sleeping well—and the true issue would have been lost.

When someone in our life is angry, frustrated, or disappointed, we can listen and be supportive, but we should never accept responsibility or blame for their emotions. If I had become upset and angry, that would have become my issue to deal with. (That is, I could have had feelings of being abused, not being appreciated, or feeling taken advantage of, etc.)

Don't Accept Others' Issues

Another example would be if you and I were having dinner and you decided to pay for the bill. If I attempt to give you money for my portion of the bill and you do not accept it, to whom does the money belong?

The answer is to me. It is still my money. Now, if someone tries to give you their anger and you do not accept it, to whom does it belong?

To them, of course. If someone tries to give you their frustration and you do not accept it, it belongs to them.

The same applies to every negative emotion. By your not accepting the emotion, there is only one person with that feeling. That is the person who needs to figure out their own issues.

Let only loving thoughts and actions
from others enter into yourself.

Taking Control

Once we realize that others' issues belong to them, we can let go. We will feel anger rise, and we can quickly shift and say, "This event is triggering a feeling memory from my past, but I am in control now." For instance, when another driver cuts us off, we can more calmly think, "This person seems to be in a hurry. I hope he arrives at his destination without hurting himself or anyone else."

We can even send that person a prayer and feel great inside. Now we have evolved.

The Pressure Model

Imagine a boiling pot of water on the stove. As the pressure builds under the lid, it needs to raise up to let out the steam.

But the key is not to blow off steam. It is to learn to *turn off the stove* so the emotion of anger is not even felt.

Until we're able to resolve each conflict through love, anger (and all other emotions based in fear) can be used as tools to learn about ourselves.

In Conclusion

Relationships, above all other human experiences, help us look at ourselves. The moment we begin to feel love and happiness within ourselves, the world will seem like a more loving and happy place.

Remember being "in love" as a teenager when everything was great? Even the things we could not stand seemed much more tolerable. The world did not change, but our internal states did. Therefore, the world seemed to be a much happier and loving place.

Remember, the perceived world is nothing more

than a reflection of ourselves. If we are standing in front of a mirror wearing a green outfit, the mirror reflects the green outfit. As soon as we change into a blue outfit, the mirror reflects the blue outfit. There is no delay, the shift is that fast. Similarly, when we make a shift in ourselves, the world changes.

> *You must take full responsibility for your emotions. You created them and, thus, you can change them. Understanding their origin will help you shift your focus.*

Once you begin to live in a happier and more loving state, all of your relationships will begin to deepen and become more intimate.

9

Reprogramming Your Subconscious Mind

Reprogramming your subconscious mind is by far the most important "technology" you can use to improve your life.

Your reprogrammed subconscious mind will guide your conscious choices to fulfill your greatest desires. You can create any future you desire.

Tap into the power of your subconscious mind and your life can reach levels beyond your wildest dreams!

Reprogram Yourself Now

Our subconscious works to keep us making the amount of money we are making and having the relationships we are having. It influences everything involving our friends, habits, emotional states, physical states, spiritual states, etc. If our lives are not the dream we once imagined, it is because of the programming of our subconscious minds.

The energy we use to keep us at the levels we are now living could just as easily elevate us to living at a dream level!

The only barrier to reaching that dream level is that our

subconscious minds have been programmed to make us believe we belong at
our current levels.

Each one of us is influenced by our
subconscious mind. The subconscious
mind represents 90 percent of our mental
power and guides our conscious mind.

Advertisers spend billions of dollars trying to influence our subconscious minds. They
know that if they convince our subconscious
minds, this will guide our conscious choices,
and—bingo—sales!

We can reprogram our subconscious images to remove the boundaries—we can become as limitless in our thoughts and creations as
the ocean or universe is vast.

Advertisements

↓↓↓ ↓↓↓

Subconscious Mind

Conscious Choices

Purchase Decisions

Human Power

To harness the power available to you, you
need to believe that you are a co-creator of the
universe.

Look around you. Everything you see—the
book, table, chairs, walls, couches, carpet, tile, pictures, TV, VCR, colors—everything was created
by humans. We first had the thought, then put the
idea into form by drawings. Then, taking more
action, we made a model, made changes, and produced the final product.

Observe the massive imagination of humankind as evidenced by lights, bridges, skyscrapers, computers, mansions, cars, boats, and on and on. We are co-creators of this world.

The discoverer of the benzene ring formulated the structure after seeing it in a dream. Many discoveries and creations are first formulated in the subconscious mind and then percolate into the conscious mind.

We have an unlimited resource of imagination that we can tap into through our subconscious minds.

Tap Your Subconscious Power

There is no difference between you and the greatest minds in this world except they believed in their ability to create—and persisted in their beliefs even against the greatest odds.

Thomas Edison persisted through almost 9,000 trials before discovering the filament that would hold a current and become a light. With Edison-like persistence, what can you or I achieve? We can achieve anything we are committed to achieving!

Keep Trying

Edison looked at creativity as simply good, honest, hard work. Genius, he once said is 99% perspiration and 1% inspiration. It took over 50,000 experiments to invent the alkaline storage cell battery and 9,000 to perfect the light bulb.

How To Program Your "Mind"

The process of change is merely reversing the limited thinking and programming of the past. Our brains are not us, just as our hearts and lungs are not us. They are all a part of us. They each have a role.

Our brains work by analyzing data. They monitor our internal states and the information from the outside

The reprogramming process for your subconscious mind is much like upgrading software in your computer. We must remove the program installed from the past and replace it with the program we want to live by.

world. Our brains help us interact with both our bodies and the external world.

Our emotional states are governed by our beliefs, our current conscious focus, and our expressions of language and physiology (the way we carry and move our bodies). Our subconscious minds affect all three areas.

Your Subconscious Believes You

Your subconscious mind silently observes everything and accepts as real everything that it comes across. There is no separation, no classifying, in the subconscious process.

Everything the subconscious mind observes is as real to it as these words are to your conscious mind. When you view a person being shot on TV, the subconscious mind has no clue that this is not you getting shot. Your conscious mind knows it is not real, but your subconscious mind doesn't.

When you dream, your subconscious mind believes what is happening is real. Therefore your body reacts to the dream. You wake up in a sweat; you are scared or excited; your heart may be pounding. The subconscious mind does not understand that a dream is not real.

The beauty of how your subconscious mind works is that reprogramming it is easy and natural.

Everything you encounter affects your subconscious mind. What you encounter can expand your subconscious mind, making it limitless and powerful—or it can do the opposite, creating false limits and fears.

How To Jump-Start Your Day

Every morning should be greeted by a series of powerful questions and affirmations. The design of these questions will focus your conscious mind on the goals or values you feel are the most important in your life. At the same time, they will send a message to your subconscious mind.

The message to your subconscious mind should be that you already are what you want to be or have the reached the goals you seek.

Remember if your subconscious mind believes you are something or have something, it will direct your conscious mind as if it were true.

Reprogramming Your Subconscious

Here is an example of communicating with your subconscious so you can better understand this concept.

Question: *"How can I have even more love in my life?"*

The question to the conscious mind is obvious. It will focus your thoughts and actions on how to achieve more love in your life. The message to the subconscious mind is that we already have love in our lives by stating *even more* love.

Even if you currently feel this is absolutely not the case, you must convince your subconscious mind that it is true. By doing this, you will guide your thoughts and actions to fulfill the image.

Proactive Questions

Here are some other powerful examples of positive questions you can ask yourself:

?
- How can I have even more happiness in my life?
- How can I have even more adventure in my life?
- How can I develop even closer relationships with my family?
- How can I create even more passion in my relationship?

?
- How can I again become a *multi*millionaire?
- How can I create even more financial abundance in my life?
- How can I feel even more gratitude/thankfulness in my life?
- How can I contribute even more to this world?

- How can I add even greater value to this world?
- How can I make my life even more peaceful and loving?
- How can I connect even more with other people?
- How can I see everyone I meet even more like my own brother or sister?

- How can I see everyone as even more like myself?
- How can I become even more connected to God/Allah/Jehovah/Shiva/Buddha/Christ/cosmic conscious, etc.?
- How can I become even more connected to people of a different race/religion/country?
- How can I treat myself even better?

- How can I love myself even more?
- How can I develop even more loving relationships with my children?
- How can I show even more respect to the fellow workers in my company?
- How can I again increase sales by threefold and enjoy the process?

- How can I make even more money with even less effort?
- How can I have even greater confidence in my skills?
- How can I become even more creative?
- How can I again create like my brother Michelangelo?

We Are All Michelangelos

"While the artists...were doing their best to imitate and to understand nature, blending every faculty to increase that high comprehension sometimes called intelligence, the Almighty Creator took pity on their often fruitless labor. He resolved to send to earth a spirit capable of supreme expression in all the arts, one able to give form to painting, perfection to sculpture, and grandeur to architecture. The Almighty Creator also graciously endowed this chosen one with an understanding of philosophy and with the grace of poetry. In the Casentino, therefore, in 1475, a son was born to Signor Lodovico di Lionardo di Buonarroti Simoni...Moved by compelling impulse, he named the boy Michelangelo."

—Giorgio Vasari,
Lives of the Painters, Sculptors, and Architects

Art From The Ruins

Michelangelo was the greatest artist in a time of greatness. His masterpiece, David, revealed his ability to do what others could not.

Back in 1463 the authorities of the cathedral of Florence acquired a sixteen-foot-high chunk of white marble to be carved into a sculpture. After two well known sculptors worked on the piece and gave up, the mangled block was put in storage. Other sculptors were asked to continue the work. They all demanded expensive new marble, special tools, and assistants. Their demands were not economically feasible, so the project was scrapped.

Forty years later, Michelangelo took the mangled block of marble from storage and carved it into the youthful, courageous "David" within eighteen months.

—Michael Michalko, author of *Thinkertoys*

We are all Michelangelos waiting to unfold. We all have this incredible creative power and spirit waiting to be ignited.

Think of our creator as the waiter or waitress in the sky wanting to fulfill our every *clear* desire. Let us become focused. Let go of the past garbage and live in the present moment of perfection.

Keep A Positive Focus

The act of asking of questions in the morning will focus your mind on your goals and shift you away from the usual disempowering thoughts or questions like:

- I can't believe I have to work this morning.
- Do I have to go to school?
- I feel so tired.
- Why does everything happen to me?

These negative thoughts reflect a subconscious image of lack or fear. It's depressing you now just to read them!

To change your life, change your messages to yourself. Integrate the powerful positive questions into your daily routine in the morning and the evening.

For even faster results, put them on cards and review them throughout the day. Think of the process as if you were creating a commercial to sell yourself on the goals you wish to achieve. You are creating a powerful advertisement to influence your conscious and subconscious mind.

Positive, goal-oriented affirmations are statements of our future goals, desires, and dreams put into present context.

Here is an example from a person making $15,000 a year: "I have a six-figure income, and love sharing it with my friends and family."

Create a series of positive goal-oriented affirmations and read them every day. One of the most powerful methods is to dictate your questions and affirmations with passion, excitement, and confidence onto a tape. Use the present tense. Then listen to this tape every day.

An example of a goal is: "I live in a 6,000-square-foot

mansion overlooking the ocean."

The more emotion, the more powerful the effect. For instance: "I love living in my 6,000 square foot mansion and eating breakfast on my balcony that overlooks the ocean." See it, feel it. Convince your subconscious mind by repetition, and remove any limiting beliefs, and you will notice dramatic shifts in your life and emotional state.

In Conclusion

Reprogramming our subconscious minds is by far the most important technology we can use to improve our lives. Our subconscious minds were programmed by our early childhood environments and experiences, and now we have the technology to create our own powerful programs.

10

Take Control Of Your Mind

We must monitor the information that enters our minds. As you recall, the subconscious mind believes that everything it experiences is real. Therefore all negative information must be limited or avoided.

Research shows that watching TV news is depressing because it focuses on negative events. For instance, people who watch more news than the average viewer, estimate that threats to their safety are far higher than they really are.

When someone is shot on TV, our subconscious minds believes we were shot. Since this is not the message we wish to send our subconscious minds, consider watching less violent programs.

Greatness In, Greatness Out!

We must become as careful of the information that enters our minds as we are with the gasoline we put into our car. Of all the millions of liquids there are in this world, we only put one in our gas tank—gasoline. Of the three or so types of gasoline, we usually select the same one. We are so consistent that many people choose a certain company's gasoline to get the "best performance."

Don't Feed Your Mind Junk

Look at the junk food some people feed their bodies and their children! And even more striking, look at what we permit to enter our minds. We must start monitoring everything that has the potential to enter our minds, from TV and newspapers, to the people with whom we associate.

> *Negativity is a straightjacket for your unlimited potential. Avoid it whenever possible. When you're exposed to it, send an even more powerful positive message to your subconscious.*

If you see someone get shot on TV as you are looking for a comedy or an inspirational program, remind your subconscious that the world has over five billion people and most of them live in peace and harmony. Guard what enters your mind with an even greater consistency than you guard what goes into your gas tank. I know I don't need to say which is more important!

TV Can Traumatize

Children are traumatized daily by TV. I provided therapy for an eight-year-old boy whom I'll call Billy. Billy had developed constipation and encopresis (having bowel movements in his pants). After several sessions, he was still unable to disclose any recent stressors or traumas.

I used the technique of talking in the third person so he would not have to discuss himself. I asked for his help in understanding a nine-year-old boy who could not go to the bathroom. I told Billy I wanted to help this nine year old but I had no idea what was wrong and asked for his help.

The Trauma

Billy then went into a twenty-minute discussion of how this nine-year-old probably watched the movie "Candy Man." In it, after a person says "Candy Man" in the mirror of the bathroom five times, a horrifying man appears with a hook for one hand and cuts the person in pieces starting between the legs!

No wonder Billy was traumatized and afraid to enter the bathroom!

After gaining this awareness, Billy and I did a few desensitization sessions and the problem was resolved. This is an obvious example of trauma that occurred on both the conscious and subconscious levels.

Being Mindful

Did you pay attention to the feelings and body sensations *you* experienced just reading about the Candy Man? Remind yourself that there are over five billion people in this world and most of them live in harmony and love.

Negative messages can be subtle—or blatant, like the above example. We must become fully aware of what we let in from the external world, to ourselves—and especially to our children.

> *We must become totally mindful of the information we let into our minds, what we say to ourselves, and the information we give out to others.*

How Can You Miss The News?

When discussing these ideas with colleagues someone invariably mentions the importance of keeping up with the news.

We don't need daily doses of the news!

I don't read the newspaper, except for possibly the business section and, at times, the sports section. I also don't watch the news. I don't even have cable TV.

I go to work (I call it play) in the morning, come home, exercise, eat and spend time with my wife, converse with friends, read, write, relax, and meditate. I am feeding my mind positive information, growing and creating, or going within myself.

Crisis Intervention

We can live without the daily reminders of all the challenging events that happen in the world.

As a psychiatric resident at the University of South Florida

Medical Center, I was part of a crisis intervention team. We would go to the business or area where a crisis took place and perform group and individual crisis intervention. The majority of the crisis intervention was in the form of support therapy helping survivors deal with loss, guilt, or whatever emotions surfaced during and after the event.

These crises were incredible experiences in learning, and an opportunity for us to give voluntarily to the community. The crises ranged from shootings and fires to Hurricane Andrew that devastated parts of South Florida.

When I was called to work on these events, I would request the latest information on the incident. I would receive the latest newspaper articles and then we would have a briefing on the most recent information. I would enter the area prepared at least as well as my colleagues for the situation at hand.

If I could do crisis intervention without the daily watching of the latest crisis on TV, do *you* really need to know the details of all the challenging events the media chooses to cover?

How We Can Change The Media

Report Card	QUARTER			
	1	2	3	4
Math	D+	B-	B+	
Social Studies	C	B-	B+	
Art	C+	B+	A -	
Science	D+	C+	A -	
Reading	C	B-	A -	
Grammar	D	B	B+	
P.E.	C+	B-	A	
Spelling	C	B-	A -	

Negativity should be less newsworthy! A fourth grader who turns his grades around from Cs and Ds to become an honor student is what can be newsworthy. Or a financially-poor student's acceptance into the college of her dreams after a long and hard struggle. Or people who have reached the smallest or greatest of achievements.

Take Control

When enough people shift to take control of what enters their minds, then we will shift the focus of the news.

There's no point in blaming the news producers. What appears on the news is based on the past responses of their viewers. They give the public what the majority of their viewers want to experience.

Model Me Great

The process of feeding our minds with humor, positivity, inspiration, and loving information will help transform our subconscious images. Remember, our subconscious minds accept everything we encounter. Therefore, in order to become our vision or reach our goals, we need to expose ourselves to the greatest talents in the fields we wish to pursue or master.

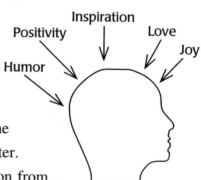

I have found great inspiration from Anthony Robbins; Wayne Dyer, PhD; and Deepak Chopra, MD. Deepak Chopra simplifies the great insight of Eastern thought. He combines the wisdom of the East with the technologies of the West. He is a leading figure in the transformation taking place in medicine in this country.

"It's never too late to have a happy child-hood."

—Bumper sticker

Consider Anthony Robbins. I have never seen an individual so full of energy, power, insight, charisma, and clarity of mind over an extended period of time as Anthony Robbins. He ignites the stage and the audience.

Listening to Wayne Dyer is almost a daily habit for me—the same tapes over and over again. He is an incredible example of the happiness, bliss, and peace of mind we can reach by going within, calming the mind, and becoming connected with the Creator.

Both of these men struggled through hard times. At times Anthony Robbins's family had no food on the table when he was growing up. Wayne Dyer's father was a heavy drinker who left the family when Wayne was a baby. Wayne lived in foster homes as a child.

More Role Models

General Norman Schwarzkopf is another example of someone who rose above early struggles, and worked through the conflicts to become one of the greatest leaders of our time.

The Challenge

In his autobiography *It Doesn't Take A Hero,* General Schwarzkopf writes about his struggle with his mother who was a heavy drinker:

I didn't like confrontations, but sometimes I fought back with sabotage: when Mom was out of the house I'd search the kitchen for the bottles of bourbon and gin, pour them out behind the garage, and smash them.

At times it was anger that overwhelmed me, at other times fear, but what I felt most often was complete helplessness. I simply retreated, which Mom let me do because I was the youngest and her favorite. Deep inside me was a place where I would withdraw when things were unhappy at home. I discovered I could hide the painful feelings and still make friends and love dogs and help old ladies across the street and be a good guy. I had lots of buddies, but no really close friend. I learned to be self-contained and independent. Maybe that was a gift my mother gave me.

Turn Challenges Into "Gifts"

General Schwarzkopf's story shows that challenges—like living with an alcoholic mother— can be a "gift." Now is a good time to rethink your own past pain. Accept the gifts that challenging events can bring, forgive the pain, and move on.

Helen Keller also dramatically turned a disadvantage into many gifts. Blind and deaf by the time she was 19

> *"Life is a bold adventure or nothing at all."*
> —Helen Keller

months old, she eventually founded the Lions Club, and achieved many other accomplishments to help others. If, throughout her struggles, Helen Keller was able to believe and realize that life is an adventure, what could possibly keep us in a state of fear?

"There is a technique, a knack, for thinking, just as there is for doing other things. You are not wholly at the mercy of your thoughts, any more than they are you. They are a machine you can learn to operate.

—Alfred North Whitehead

Rise Above Events

Everyone has strug–gles and challenges. That is what life is about. The people who achieve their full potential work through the struggles and challenges. They see life as a gift, not an excuse on which to blame their fears.

Find your role models in whatever area of life you wish to master. Absorb what you need. Listen to tapes, read inspiring books, and avoid the negative messages that are constantly barraging our minds.

It's Time To Take Control

For us to reprogram our subconscious minds, we must take control—become mindful—of everything that enters and exits. We no longer need to live from past beliefs or habits. We can create new and empowering ones.

Analyze everything. If it is not consistent with your life's mission and goals, eliminate it whenever possible.

Each day, I'm learning to love life even more: people, my work, each day, each moment. But it has not always been this way for me. It takes time and a commitment to yourself. Remember, the more gifts we can let unfold through ourselves, the more we can give to all those around us and the world. Limiting ourselves limits those around us.

Seek Positive People

Another aspect of changing our lives is to evaluate our relationships. The "vibrations" of our friends, colleagues, and co-workers whom we are around each day affect us. We may need to spend less time with those who always represent themselves as victims in situations, or who think negatively about life's events.

In Chapter 5, I wrote about the negative subconscious image, and how we could easily tell if a person had such an image. Becoming mindful of everything we let into our minds also means the people with whom we associate. Unless people with whom we interact are on the path to personal development, self-awareness, and self-mastery, we will feel ourselves being drained or pulled down by their negativity.

> *Be around only those people who think you are*
> *special and gifted.*

You are special and gifted, and these people are seeing the true you. We should all begin to envision others as even more than they see themselves so that they can become this greater vision of themselves. We need to do this, especially with children.

Visualize For Victory

Visualization is another tool we can use to reprogram our subconscious minds. Visualize yourself being and doing exactly what you desire to become.

Imagine you are there doing the things, feeling the emotions, and living the life of the person you envision. Integrate those feelings and thoughts totally into your body. We are spirit, mind, and body. All parts must be integrated for us to be fully integrated individuals.

Our bodies must be involved with this reprogramming. Think about how depressed people look. Their shoulders, eyes, and heads are downward. Their bodies droop, and movements are slow and labored. Their voices are slow and in monotone. The body is slower to heal from medical illnesses when a person is in a state of depression and there is an increased risk for disease, especially infections.

Excited, confident people appear with their heads up, shoulders back, and bright looks on their faces. Their movements are directed, powerful, and fast.

Mind-Body Connections

How about the word "psychoneuroimmuno-endocrine" system? It simply means that our minds and bodies are connected.

Begin the process now of integrating your physiology with your new belief system. Develop the posture and physical expressions of the person you wish to become. You will immediately be that way.

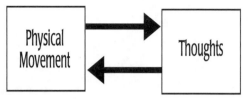

Visualize the posture and expressions in your mind and feel the confidence and certainty. How many great leaders can you recall who appeared hunched over, moving slowly with their eyes and heads directed downward? Position your body as if you were already living your dreams.

Every thought you have has a physical manifestation. The reverse is also true. Change your posture and the way you walk, and you will change your thoughts and, therefore, your life.

Positive Thinking And Physiology

Every negative thought influences your body and increases the level of stress-related hormones such as cortisol. Negative thoughts can increase blood pressure and heart rate, and reduce breathing effectiveness. Over time these can be physically harmful.

The opposite is also true. Positive, loving thoughts relax the body, open the body up, slow the heart rate, deepen the breathing, and lower blood pressure and cortisol.

Thoughts also affect the neurochemicals of the brain. Medical research documents brain function through the use of PET scans, which measure the metabolism of radioactively labeled glucose. These studies have shown that cognitive "talk" therapy, which focuses on changing the belief system, produces an increase in function in areas of the brain similar to the response to antidepressant medication.

In other words, just as antidepressants can change the neurochemicals of your brain, so can changing your belief system. To take this to the next step, very negative and abusive environments or thoughts can create an unhealthy shift in the neurochemicals in your brain, producing negative emotions.

Condition Yourself Positively

Ivan Petrovich Pavlov was a Russian physiologist and Nobel Prize winner. His famous "Pavlov's dogs" experiment demonstrated learned conditioning. It is also an example of the mind/body connection.

In the experiment, a hungry dog was shown a dish of food, and at the same time the experimenters rang a bell. The dog salivated at the sight of the food and, at the same time, heard the bell.

This pairing of food and bell was done repeatedly. Eventually, just ringing the bell caused the dog to salivate. The dog's beliefs were conditioned so that the bell meant food and this association translated into salivation.

We must integrate our bodies with the process of reconditioning our conscious and subconscious minds. Our minds and bodies are connected. We can use this fact to our advantage.

Going For The Gold—Goal Setting

We must all focus our minds on the solutions and goals we desire in life. We need to write goals for each aspect of our lives—physical, emotional, intellectual, financial, and spiritual. I highly recommend that you integrate all these areas in your long-term goals.

Write Out 6-mo., 1-yr., 3-yr., and 5-yr. Goals

1. Physical
2. Emotional
3. Financial
4. Relationships
5. Spiritual
6. Educational

Write Down Your Goals

By writing goals down, we focus our minds on the solutions and away from the constant rehashing of the problems.

> *We attract to ourselves the thoughts*
> *we are pondering most intensely.*

We can increase our solution-focus by writing out the dreams or goals we desire. It also helps to write down why we desire those goals and an action plan.

Take Action!

Then, most importantly, we must take action. There are many goal-setting seminars in this country and around the world. Goals prepare our minds to recognize the opportunities that can help us create our visions.

Modified Serenity Prayer

God, grant me the courage to change the things I can change, accept the things I cannot change, the wisdom to know the difference, and the will to take action.

(unknown)

Goals Focus Us

At this very moment, your body is receiving trillions of messages from both inside and outside yourself.

We have learned to close off most of these stimuli and focus our attentions. If we are angry, we focus on what seems to justify this emotion in the current moment. If we set goals and review them daily, our minds will be ready to focus on what will achieve these goals.

All the information that crosses our awareness will now be considered through that filter of goals. You will be able to select the opportunities that will help you along your path. Without this focus, you would have missed many opportunities that will help you.

Goal setting is vital. (My wife and I will soon be releasing a goal-setting series, but please do not wait. Get started now!)

Help Focus Children Early

In closing this chapter there are two questions that every parent absolutely must learn to ask their children every night before they fall asleep. We must also *listen* to their responses. If we practice this, our relationships with our children will be incredible.

- What did you learn today?
- Who did you love today?

Listen, I love you (kiss) goodnight.

In Conclusion

Taking control of our minds will change our lives. Start today and you will see results immediately.

CHAPTER 11

The End Is Just The Beginning

A concerned father asked his son's teacher, "Which profession should my son pursue?" The teacher responded, "It doesn't matter. He'll never make a success of anything."

The father was Herman Einstein and his son was Albert Einstein! Albert was a slow learner as a child and many felt he was not as intelligent as the other children. We are all grateful that Albert did not buy into those beliefs!

In this book, we have come along way together, learning many ways to understand ourselves and how to make great shifts in our lives.

I have not always been excited and happy about my life. By looking at my rules and rewriting them, changing old disempowering beliefs, and accepting responsibility for every emotion I experience, I have empowered myself. Now I experience life as a tremendous joy and an exciting adventure.

Commit To Growth

We must commit to seeing life as a growth process. We are either moving forward—becoming more loving, caring, giving, and compassionate—or moving backward, becoming more angry, frustrated, disappointed, and isolated.

Every thought, word, and action is based in love or fear. We can all help our world by making a shift in ourselves and by teaching others with our examples. We can all learn by asking better questions and looking within ourselves.

> "Sin is the absence of love."
>
> *—A Course In Miracles*

We have looked at becoming mindful of every thought we have, every thought we share and permit into our minds. I discussed some effective parenting techniques and how to become an incredible role model. We learned how to increase the intellectual potential of our children and, at the same time, instill powerful and positive character traits.

You read about Jason, Jessica, Jennifer, Steve, Sara, and Mary who have been great teachers for us all. Through them, we learned about the conscious and subconscious mind, our belief systems, and how to influence them instead of being controlled by them.

Emotions have always been felt, yet rarely understood. I know you have a better understanding of emotions now and also how to shift them in an instant.

Good Lessons Are Everywhere

We are all geniuses, each having roles and missions in this world. We are all courageous and great lovers, carrying inside the ability to transcend our instinct to survive to risk our lives to save others. All of these great things are within us! Sometimes it is just a matter of getting out of the way by removing the ego and living in the moment as a child.

My wife, Susan, and I were eating brunch at a local restaurant. Alongside our table was a family with a four-year-old boy who was enjoying the moment playing with sugar bags and his silverware. The waitress came over to the table and began to announce the children's menu, "Today we have grilled cheese and fries." Immediately the boy excitedly yelled, "Grilled cheese and fries, grilled cheese and fries!"

His father, after looking around

the restaurant, calmly stated, "Billy, now wait until the waitress is finished telling you the menu." The waitress then replied, "We also have a peanut butter and jelly sandwich with grapes." Billy immediately yelled at the top of his lungs, "Peanut butter and jelly and grapes." With this outburst of enthusiasm, his father and mother replied to the waitress, "We will take the peanut butter and jelly sandwich with grapes."

Your Better Future

Billy's response was excited, enthusiastic, spontaneous, and totally in the moment. Our children have great lessons to teach us—like the value of being in the moment, living in a state of love, forgiving, and picking ourselves up after a fall and enthusiastically returning back to play. I have read many great books and listened to many tapes. **My life shifted when I decided to take action and apply the ideas to my life**.

Let us put fear away! Only one effective idea needs to be put into action to take your life to the next level.

Thank you for joining me on this incredible journey. May the knowledge and experiences I have shared with you continue to enrich your life and the lives of those you touch.

Please contact me with your own stories and feedback. Then I'll inform you about new material because we can all help create a better world through brilliant babies and powerful adults.

References

Adamson-Macedo, Elvidina N., Dattani, Ilesh, Wilson, Ann, & deCarvalho, F.A. (1993). A small sample follow-up study of children who received tactile stimulation after preterm birth: Intelligence and achievements. Special Issue: Prenatal and perinatal behaviour. *Journal of Reproductive and Infant Psychology,* Vol. 11 (3), 165-168.

Beck, A.T. (1979). *Cognitive Therapy and the Emotional Disorders.* New York: International Universities Press.

Begley, Sharon. (1996). Your Child's Brain. *Newsweek,* February 19, pp. 55-61.

Brooks-Gunn, Jeanne, McCaton, Cecilia M., Casekly Patrick; McCormick, Marie C. et al. (1994). Early intervention in low-birth-weight premature infants. Results through age 5 years from the Infant Health and Development Program. *Journal of the American Medical Association,* Vol. 272 (16), 1257-1262.

Cary, Emily P. Music as a prenatal and early childhood impetus to enhancing intelligence and cognitive skills. (1987). *Roeper Review,* Vol. 9 (3), 155-158.

Cassidy, Ann (1996). The Power of Music. *Working Mother,* May, pp. 47-51.

Chopra, Deepak. (1997). *The Spirit of Love: 11 Spiritual Lessons for Creating the Love You Want.* New York: Dutton.

Clark, Ronald A. (1971). *Einstein, The Life and Times.* New York: World Publishing Co. pp 22 & 27.

Coleman, Daniel. (1995). *Emotional Intelligence: Why It Can Matter More than IQ.* New York: Bantam Books.

Detterman, D.K., & Sternberg, Robert J. (1982). *How and How Much Can Intelligence Be Increased?* Norwood, NJ: Ablex, 1982.

Dossey, Larry. (1993). *Healing Words, The Power of Prayer and the Practice of Medicine.* New York: HarperSanFrancisco, pp. 179-192.

Dyer, Wayne W. (1985). *What Do You Really Want for Your Children?* New York: Morrow.

Fifer, W.P. & Moon, Co. (1989). Psychobiology of Newborn Auditory Preferences. *Seminars in Perinatology,* Vol. 13, 430-433.

Huttunen, M.O., & Niskanen, P. (1978). Prenatal loss of father and psychiatric disorders. Archives of General Psychiatry, Vol. 35 (4), 429-431.

Jampolsky, Gerald G. (1979). *Love is Letting Go Of Fear.* Berkeley: Celestial Arts.

Jung, Carl G. (1964). *Man And His Symbols.* London: Aldus Books, Limited.

Kaplan, Harold I., & Sadock, Benjamin J. (1988). *Synopsis of Psychiatry: Behavior Sciences; Clinical Psychiatry* (5th Ed.). Baltimore: Williams & Wilkins, p. 94.

Montessori, Maria. (1967). *The Absorbent Mind.* New York: Dell Publishing Co.

O'Keefe, Garrett J., & Reid-Nash, Kathaleen. (1987). Crime News and Real-World Blues: The Effect of the Media on Social Reality, *Communication Research,* Vol. 14 (2), 147-163.

Ornstein, Robert, & Thompson, Richard F. (1984). *The Amazing Brain.* Boston: Houghton Mifflin.

Plato (translated by Francis MacDonald Cornfield) 1941. *The Republic of Plato*. London. Oxford University Press. pp. 88-90.

Prabhupada, A.C. Bhaktivedanta Swami . (1968). *Bhagavad-Gita As It Is*. New York: The Bhaktivedanta Book Trust. Chapter 10, p. 166.

Ramo, Joshua Cooper. (1993). Music Soothes the Savage Brain: Does Mozart Make You Smarter? *Newsweek,* October 25, 51.

Rauscher, Frances H. (1994). Tuning Up Young Brains. *Science News,* Aug 27, Vol. 146, 143.

Rauscher, Frances H. & Shaw, PhD, Gordon L. (1994). Learning Keys: Music May Give Kids' Minds a Head Start. *Prevention,* Feb, p. 24(2).

Rauscher, Frances H., Shaw, Gordon L., 7 Ky, Katerine N. Music and spatial task performance. (1993). *Nature,* Vol 365, 611.

Robbins, Anthony. (1991). *Awaken the Giant Within: How to Take Immediate Control of Your Mental, Emotional, Physical, & Financial Destiny*. New York: Fireside.

Sagan, Carl (1980). *Cosmos*. New York: Ballantine Books. p. 2.

Schneider, Michael S. (1994). *A Beginner's Guide to Constructing the Universe: The Mathematical Archetypes of Nature, Art, and Science*. New York: Harper Perennial, p. 284.

Schucman, Helen. (1975). *A Course In Miracles*. Mill Valley: Foundation for Inner Peace.

Seligman, Martin E.P., with Reivich, Karen, Jaycox, Lisa, and Gillham, Jane. (1995). *The Optimistic Child: A Revolutionary Program That Safeguards Children Against Depression and Builds Lifelong Resilience*. Boston: Houghton-Mifflin.

Siegel, Bernie S. (1986). *Love, Medicine, and Miracles*. Harper Perennial.

Stattin, Hakan, Klackenberg-Larsson, Ingrid. (1993). Early language and intelligence development and their relationship to future criminal behavior. *Journal of Abnormal Psychology,* Vol. 102 (2), 369-378.

Sternberg, Robert J. (1984). How Can We Teach Intelligence? *Educational Leadership,* pp. 38-48.

The New American Bible, St. Joseph Edition. *New Testament, John.* New York: Catholic Book Publishing Co. Chapter 1, verse 1-16.

*The New American Bible, New Testament, John, Ch*apter 8, verse 3-8.

van Izendoorn, Marinus, H., & Van Vliet-Visser, Sita. (1988). The Relationship Between Quality of Attachment in iInfancy and IQ in Kindergarten. *Journal of Genetic Psychology,* Vol. 149 (1), 23-28.

van Ijzendoorn, Marinus H., Dijkstra, Jarissa, & Bus, Adriana G, Univ. of Leiden, Ctr. for Child & Family Studies, Netherlands (1995). Attachment, Intelligence, and Language: A Meta-analysis. *Social Development*, July, Vol. 4 (2), pp. 115-128.

Verny, Thomas, & Kelly, John. (1981). The Secret Life of the Unborn Child. New York: Dell Publishing Co.

Wasik, Barbara H., Ramey, Craig T., Bryant, Donna M., & Sparling, Joseph J. (1990). A Longitudinal Atudy of Two Early Intervention Atrategies: Project CARE. *Child Development,* Vol. 61 (6), 1682-1696.

Index